Contemporary Spoken Persian

A Self-Instructional Course

Book 1

by

Mehdi Marashi

 An Audio-Cassette Program

Especially created to accompany this book are 8 instructional audio cassettes. They are available from the publisher.

AUDIO·FORUM

Division of
JEFFREY NORTON PUBLISHERS, INC.

Guilford, CT

CONTEMPORARY SPOKEN PERSIAN, A SELF-INSTRUCTIONAL
COURSE, VOLUME 1, BY MEHDI MARASHI

ISBN: 0-88432-132-0

Typesetting: CACI Language Center
1815 North Fort Myer Drive, Arlington, VA   22209

Cover Design: Persian calligraphy

Published by Audio Forum,
a division of Jeffrey Norton Publishers, Inc.
On-The-Green, Guilford, CT   06437

London Sales Office: 31 Kensington Church St.,
London   W8 4LL U.K.

CONTENTS

CONTENT GUIDE FOR TAPES

ACKNOWLEDGMENTS

Colleagues whose advice, ideas, and collaboration are reflected in this book would make a long list. I acknowledge with pleasure my indebtedness to all of them, and in particular to Professors M. A. Jazayery (University of Texas at Austin), Mahmoud Taba Tabaie (Defense Language Institute, Monterey, California), William Royce (Arizona State University), Ray Freeze (University of Utah), and Jalil Hazratguluv and his well-qualified associates (Persian Department, Tashkent State University).

In acknowledging my indebtedness to my supervisors at the University of Utah who persuaded me to develop this material, I should mention Professor Stephan Durrant, Chairman of the Department of Languages, and Professor Lee Bean, Director of the Middle East Center. Typing the manuscript, consistency of format, and xeroxing the lessons were the contributions of the competent staff of the Middle East Center to whom I acknowledge my sincere gratitude.

My thanks to the students of Persian at the University of Utah who participated in the tryouts of this course. Their valuable suggestions made the content and format of the lessons more suitable for teaching and learning spoken Persian.

I am especially grateful to Mrs. Latifeh Haghighi and Mr. Woody Trathen, whose assistance in the preparation, review, editing, and recording of the material was invaluable.

M. M.

PREFACE

Contemporary Spoken Persian, a self-instructional course designed to teach the spoken language, emphasizes practical use of the language and comprehension. These are the communication skills most commonly needed and most readily acquired.

Both the audio cassettes (8) and the accompanying text for Contemporary Spoken Persian have been planned to give specific guidance to the self-learner. Native speakers on the audio cassettes provide authentic models in carefully constructed exercises and drills for the self-learner to imitate and repeat in the pauses provided between sentences. Lesson units include dialogs, vocabulary, and in some instances self-tests. The text is entirely in transcription; Persian script is not introduced. A key to the exercises and self-tests, and an English-Persian glossary are found at the end of the text. Grammatical explanations are kept to a minimum and provided only when necessary for the understanding of specific text material.

The language of the course is that of contemporary speech used in everyday situations that a foreigner would be likely to encounter with speakers of Persian or when visiting Iran today. Therefore, the language acquired represents the appropriate use of Persian in culturally authentic situations.

Today more Westerners are learning Persian to aid work or research in various fields such as engineering, history, anthropology, political science, sociology, and archeology. The development of this course is the result of several years of experience in teaching Persian to American college students and Peace Corps volunteers, and in supervising individuals learning Persian through the correspondence course offered by the Division of Continuing Education at the University of Utah. Thus, Contemporary Spoken Persian is the beneficiary of many field tests and numerous comments from these students of the past. The author hopes that this present work will aid the individual self-learner in speaking and understanding the Persian of today.

Mehdi Marashi
September 14, 1985

KEY TO PRONUNCIATIONS AND
ABBREVIATIONS

The symbols used in transcriptions have values similar to their English values, except as follows:

Symbols	Persian	
/æ/	/sǽr/	head
/e/	/yék/	one
/o/	/dó/	two
/a/	/bád/	wind
/u/	/xúb/	good
/i/	/míz/	desk
/š/	/šám/	dinner
/ž/	/žǽrf/	deep
/c/	/cáp/	print
/'/	/bǽ'd/	later
/x/	/xúb/	good
/q/	/qælǽm/	pen

In words of more than one syllable, the stressed syllable is marked with an accent, placed over the vowel.

The comma (,) marks an intonational unit, usually a complete sentence or part of it.

The colon (:) after vowels indicates the vowel length.

Persian expressions are given in the transcription system adopted by American linguists and the Center for Applied Linguistics in Washington, D.C.

Persian sounds with no counterpart in English that may cause some difficulty to speakers of English, have been described in English in the book. Systematic practice has also been provided for recognition and production of sounds and sound patterns of Persian.

Dialogs are followed by explanatory notes in English and a variety of pronunciation exercises. These exercises, which are to be used with each unit, have been specially designed to increase your ability in understanding and speaking Persian.

Abbreviations

Adj	adjective
Adv	adverb
Aux	auxiliary
Comp	complement
Mod	modifier
Neg	negative
N	noun
NP	noun phrase
Pl	plural
Prev	pre-verb
PPart	past participle
Sg	singular
Vb	verb
VP	verb phrase
1 pers	first person

DIALOG ONE

Vocabulary

sælám [1]	hello
hál	condition, health
cetówr	how
xúb	fine, good
mérsi	thanks
šomá	you
bǽd	bad
níst	is not
xodá haféz	good-bye
besælamǽt	good-bye
šǽb bexéyr	I wish you good night.
sób bexéyr	Good morning.
lótfe šomá ziyád	Good-bye (lit. your favor may increase).

---

[1] /sælám/ is a greeting expression which is used any time during the day. Thus, it corresponds to the English expressions: good morning, good afternoon, good evening, good day, hi, hello. The same expression may be used in response.

Greeting

sælám	Hello.
sælám, háletun cetówre?	Hello, How are you?
xúbe, mérsi, hále šomá cétowre?	Fine, thanks, and how are you?
bǽd níst, motsækkéræm.	Not bad. Thanks.

Leave-taking Expressions

For more expressions of greeting and leave-taking, see Appendix Section A.

xodá haféz	Good-bye.
besælamǽt	So long.

PRONUNCIATION (vowels; /a/ and /æ/)

Persian has six vowels, all of which have appeared in the first dialog. Note the occurrence of the vowels in the words given.

Vowels	Key Words	
/i/	/níst/	is not
/e/	/besælamǽt/	good-bye
/æ/	/bǽd/	bad
/a/	/hál/	condition
/o/	/šomá/	you
/u/	/xúb/	good

Pronunciation Drill 1

Listen to the Persian vowels: /i/e/æ/a/o/u/

Listen to the following words carefully, paying particular attention to the pronunciation of the vowels.

2

/sí/	/míz/
/sé/	/ésm/
/sǽd/	/cǽnd/
/cár/	/aqá/
/nóh/	/kót/
/punzdǽh/	/dúst/

The vowel /a/ is similar to the English vowel that occurs in hot, hall, but the lips are not rounded.
The vowel /æ/ is more or less similar to the English vowel in bad, man, cat, etc.

Pronunciation Drill 2

/dár/	/dǽr/
/sád/	/sǽd/
/kár/	/kǽr/
/xám/	/xǽm/
/lám/	/lǽm/
/cáp/	/cǽp/
/mást/	/mǽst/
/dášt/	/dǽšt/

Repeat the following pairs of words. The first word you hear in each pair contains the vowel /a/, and the second contains /æ/:

/dár/	/dǽr/
/sád/	/sǽd/
/kár/	/kǽr/
/xám/	/xǽm/
/lám/	/lǽm/
/cáp/	/cǽp/
/mást/	/mǽst/
/dášt/	/dǽšt/

DIALOG TWO

Vocabulary

ín	this
ketáb	book
ún	that
dǽftær	notebook
medád	pencil
gǽc	chalk
bǽle	yes
næxéyr	no
hǽm	also
yá	or
kaqǽz	paper
kíf	handbag, purse
eynǽk	eyeglasses
qælǽm	pen
sa'ǽt	watch, clock
keravát	tie
sændælí	chair
divár	wall
pakkón	eraser
dæstmál	handkerchief

4

In the Classroom

ín cíye?	What is this?
ún ketábe.	That is a book.
ín cíye?	What is this?
ún dæftǽre.	That is a notebook.
ín medáde?	Is this a pencil?
bǽle, ún medáde.	Yes. That is a pencil.
ín hǽm medáde?	Is this also a pencil?
næxéyr, ún medád níst, gǽce.	No, that is not a pencil; it is a piece of chalk.
ín cíye?	What is this?
ín míze.	This is a desk.
ún cíye?	What is that?
ún sændælíye.	That is a chair.
ín hǽm sændælíye?	Is this a chair also?
bǽle.	Yes.
ín míze yá sændælíye?	Is this a chair or a table?
ín míze	This is a table.
ín sændælíye?	Is this a chair?
bǽle in sændælíye.	Yes, this is a chair.
ín hǽm sændælíye?	Is this also a chair?
bǽle.	Yes.

ín ketábe yá dæftǽre?	Is this a book or a notebook?
ún ketábe.	That is a notebook.
ín medáde yá gǽce?	Is this a pencil or a piece of chalk?
ún medáde.	That is a pencil.
ún dǽre yá diváre?	Is that a door or a wall?
ún dǽre.	That is a door.
ín cíye?	What is this?
ín diváre.	This is a wall.

YES-NO QUESTIONS

This is a type of question that anticipates a /bǽle/ 'yes' or /næxéyr/ 'no' reply. In this type of question, only the intonation is inverted. (The falling intonation of the statement changes into rising intonation in this type of question.) The word order remains exactly the same as in the statement.

Pattern Drill 1

QUESTION	STATEMENT		QUESTION	STATEMENT
1. _____	_____	7. _____	_____
2. _____	_____	8. _____	_____
3. _____	_____	9. _____	_____
4. _____	_____	10. _____	_____
5. _____	_____	11. _____	_____
6. _____	_____	12. _____	_____

6

	QUESTION	STATEMENT	QUESTION	STATEMENT
13.	_____	_____	15. _____	_____
14.	_____	_____		

'OR' QUESTIONS

In this type of question, the conjunction /yá/ 'or' indicates
a choice between two or more options:

ín ketábe yá dæftǽre?   Is this a book or a notebook?

Each sentence of this type is actually a combination of more
than one basic pattern. The above sentence is equivalent to
two basic sentences.

Pattern Drill 2

Practice the variant /e/ of 'to be'. Substitute each pair of
the following expressions in the pattern for the underlined
words in the pattern.

Pattern: in ketábe ya dæftǽre?

1. /kót, keravát/
2. /dǽr, divár/
3. /míz, sændælí/
4. /dæftær, ketáb/
5. /gǽc, pakkón/

Notice that the verb 'to be'--/e/ that you hear at the end of
the sentences--does not receive stress. In the above sentences
stress falls on the last syllable of the noun preceding the
verb 'to be'.

7

Look at the pictures. Then give answers to each of the questions you hear during the pause given.

DIALOG THREE

Vocabulary

bébæxšĭd [3]	excuse me
aqá	Mr., gentleman
xanóm [4]	Miss, Mrs., lady
koja'í	from where?
hǽstæm	I am
hǽstid	you are
farsí	Persian
šĭmí	chemistry
fizík	physics
míxunæm	I study
dúst	friend
kudúm	which
iraní	Iranian

Introduction (I)

bébǽxšĭd aqá, ésme šomá cíye?	Excuse me, sir, what is your name?

---

[3] The polite expression, /bébæxšĭd/ (lit. that you forgive) may have two English equivalents:
(a) 'excuse me' (if pronounced with a drop in pitch)
(b) 'I beg your pardon' (if pronounced with a rise at the end)

[4] For more explanations, see "Titles of Address", p. 37.

ésme mǽn jáne.	My name is John.
šomá koja'í hǽstid?	Where are you from?
mǽn amrika'í hǽstæm.	I am an American.
cí míxunid?	What are you studying?
farsíyo šimí míxunæm.	I am studying Persian and chemistry.
dúste šomá cí míxune?	What does your friend study?
kudúm dústæm?	Which friend?
dúste iranítun aqáye færšád.	Your Iranian friend Mr. Farshad.
išún engelisíyo fizík míxune.	He studies English and Physics.

Introduction (II) [5]

bébæxšíd xanóm, ésme šomá cíye?	Excuse me, Miss, what is your name?
ésme mǽn barbarást.	My name is Barbara.
šomá amrika'í hǽstid?	Are you an American?
bǽle, mǽn amrika'í hǽstæm.	Yes, I am an American.
dúste šomá koja'íye?	Where is your friend from?
kudúm dústæm?	Which friend?
færhád.	Farhad.
išún iraníye.	He is an Iranian.

---

[5] For additional expressions of introduction and courtesy see Appendix Section A.

PRONUNCIATION (Vowels /e/ and /i/ and the diphthong /ey/)

The vowel /i/ is pronounced like the English vowel that occurs in seat, beet, he, receive, etc.

The Persian /e/ matches the /e/ of such English words as bet, met, ten, measure quite closely.

The diphthong /ey/, which is the combination of the vowel /e/ and the semivowel /y/, is similar to the English diphthong in such words as made, shade, rain, etc.

Pronunciation Drill 3

/sé/	/sí/
/téz/	/tíz/
/ké/	/kí/
/sén/	/sín/
/šén/	/šín/

Repetition

/sé/	/sí/
/téz/	/tíz/
/ké/	/kí/
/sén/	/sín/
/šén/	/šín/

Minimal pairs with /e/ and /ey/

/sél/	/séyl/
/zéd/	/zéyd/
/ké/	/kéy/
/ré/	/réy/
/sér/	/séyr/

Try to pronounce the following words. Substitute the vowel /i/ for the diphthong /ey/.

/kéyf/	/téyr/
/béyn/	/déyr/
/séyr/	/néyl/
/méyl/	/qéyr/

DIALOG FOUR

Vocabulary

bébæxšid [1]	I beg your pardon.
doróst	correct
halá	now
ním	half
o	and
bé	to, according to
išún	they
rób'	quarter
dæqiqé	minute

Numerals (1-12)

/yék/	1	/hǽft/	7
/dó/	2	/hǽšt/	8
/sé/	3	/nóh/	9
/cár/	4	/dǽh/	10
/pǽnj/	5	/yazdǽh/	11
/šíš/	6	/dævazdǽh/	12

Telling the Time

sa'ǽt [6] cǽnde?	What time is it?
bébæxšid?	I beg your pardon?

12

sa'ǽt cǽnde?	What time is it?
sa'ǽt nóhe.	It is nine o'clock.
doróste, sa'ǽt nóhe.	That's right, it is nine.
halá sa'ǽt cǽnde?	What time is it now?
sa'ǽt dǽhe.	It is 10:00.
halá nóh-o-níme?	Is it now 9:30?
bǽle, nóh-o-níme.	Yes, is it 9:30.
bé sa'ǽte šomá cǽnde?	What time do you have?
bé sa'ǽte mǽn nóh-o-rób'e.	9:15.
bé sa'ǽte išún cǽnde?	What time does he have?
nóh-o-bíst dæqiqǽ:st. [7]	9:20.

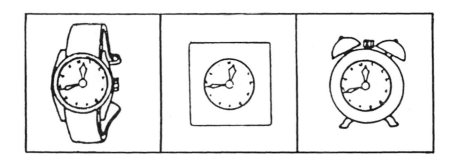

---

[6] The expression /sa'ǽt/ may mean watch, clock, time, hour.

[7] Additional expressions of time are given in Appendix Section A.

QUESTION-WORD QUESTIONS

In this type of question, which contains one of a limited number of "question-words," the speaker asks for information. Among the common question-words are:

/cé/, /cí/	what
/kojá/	where
/kí/	who
/kéy/	when
/kųdúm/	which
/cænd/	how much, how many
/cetówr/	how
/céra/	why

Pattern Drill 3

(Oral translation, using the question-words.)

Questions	Cues
1. What is the name of that gentleman?	Parviz
2. What is the name of your friend?	Robert
3. What is the name of this book?	taríxe iran
4. How is this book?	xúb
5. How is Sara?	xúb
6. What is that?	ketáb
7. What is this?	sa'ǽt
8. What time is it?	dǽh

14

VARIANTS OF THE VERB 'TO BE'

In spoken Persian, the present tense of 'to be' (third person singular) has three variants. The variants are determined by the type of sound which may precede the verb 'to be' in a sentence.

The variant /e/ 'is' is used when the word to which 'to be' is suffixed ends in a consonant:

   ín ketábe

   ín míze

The variant /æst/ 'is' is the only form of the verb 'to be' in written Persian. In spoken Persian it is used after a word which ends in the vowel /e/, e.g., /dæqiqé/ 'minute':

   sa'æt dǽho pǽnj dæqiqǽ:st   It is five after ten.

Pattern Drill 4

Substitute the following time expressions in the pattern, using the appropriate form of the verb 'to be.'

   Pattern: bê sa'ǽte mǽn hæft-o-níme.

7:20	4:00
7:15	1:05
8:10	2:45
8:30	

15

The third variant is /-st/ 'is':

ésme išun Minast

ésme išun Holakust

In these sentences, the variant /-st/ is suffixed to Holaku and Mina because of the final sounds /a/ and /u/.

Pattern Drill 5

Substitute the following names in the patterns, using the appropriate form of the verb 'to be'.

Pattern 1:   ésme ún aqá fereydúne.
  Substitute: nadér   xosró
                   færhád   borzú
                   holakú   siná
                   kiyá   hušæng
                   hormóz

Pattern 2:   ésme ín xanóm mæryǽme.
  Substitute: pærvín   ferešté
                   rowšænæk   royá
                   færzané   mæhín
                   miná   nahíd

SELF-TEST 1

Listening Comprehension
You will hear a series of Persian words. Identify the vowel sounds by numbering them. Assign number 1 to /a/ and 2 to /æ/:

1. _____   6. _____

2. _____   7. _____

3. _____   8. _____

4. _____   9. _____

5. _____

Listen to the following questions and answers. Each question will be followed by three answers. Circle A, B, or C according to whether the best answer to the question is the first, second, or third one you hear.

1	A	B	C
2	A	B	C
3	A	B	C
4	A	B	C
5	A	B	C

6	A	B	C
7	A	B	C
8	A	B	C
9	A	B	C
10	A	B	C

Vocabulary

1. _____   6. _____

2. _____   7. _____

3. _____   8. _____

4. _____   9. _____

5. _____   10. _____

True-False Questions

1. _____ There are five vowels in Persian.

2. _____ The distinction between /a/ and /æ/ is significant in Persian.

3. _____ The Persian vowel /a/ is pronounced exactly like its English counterpart.

4. _____ 'Yes-no' questions have a rising intonation.

5. _____ Word order is the same in both statements and 'yes-no' questions.

6. _____ 'Or' questions are combinations of more than one basic pattern.

7. _____ The variant of the verb 'to be' /e/ that appears at the end of a sentence receives stress.

8. _____ The pronunciation of /ké/ 'that' is different from /kéy/ 'when' because of the initial sound.

9. _____ In question-word questions, the speaker asks for information.

10. _____ Question words are limited in number.

11. _____ The variants of the verb 'to be' are determined by the type of sound which may precede the verb 'to be.'

12. _____ The variant /-e/ 'is' is used after a word that ends with a consonant.

13. _____ In spoken Persian /æst/ 'is' may be used after a word which ends in the vowel /e/.

14. _____ The variant /-st/ 'is' may follow a word that ends in either /a/ or /u/.

15. _____ The conjunction /yá/ is used in question-word questions.

16. _____ /sælám/ is a greeting expression which may correspond to a few expressions in English including 'good morning', 'good day', 'good afternoon', 'hello.'

17. _____ Persian and English have the same number of vowels.

18. _____ /šǽb bexéyr/ is a leave-taking expression. [8]

_____

[8] See the correct answers on p. 103.

18

DIALOG FIVE

Vocabulary

xanóm	Miss, Mrs., lady
danešjú	student
hǽstid	you are
míšnasid	you know (somebody)
koja'í	from where?
ésme kucɪk	first name
(ésme) famíl	family name

míšnasæm	mídunæm	I know
míšnasi	míduni	you know
míšnase	mídune	he/she knows
míšnasim	mídunim	we know
míšnasid	mídunid	you know
míšnænd	mídunænd	they know

Introduction

sælám xanóm.	sælám aqá
háletun xúbe?	mérsi, bǽd níst.
ésme šomá cíye?	ésme mǽn pæríye.
šomá danešjú hǽstid?	bǽle, danešjú hǽstæm.
ín aqá hæm danešjúst?	bǽle, išún hæm danešjúst.
ín xanóm cetówr?	išún hæm danešjúst.
šomá išún-o míšnasid	bæle, išún dúste mæne.
ésme išún cíye?	barbarást.
barbará koja'íye?	amrika'íye.
dúste išún koja'íye?	iraníye.
ésme dúste barbará cíye?	pærvíze.

PRONUNCIATION (Vowels /o/, /u/, and the diphthong /ow/)

The Persian /o/ is similar to the first part of the English vowel nucleus in so, know, coat, etc. Notice that the Persian /o/ is a "pure" sound whereas its English counterpart is pronounced /ów/, that is, the vowel /o/ followed by the semi-vowel /w/.

The vowel /u/ matches the English vowel in cool, suit, blue, etc. In pronouncing /u/ the lips are more rounded than for /o/.

Pronunciation Drill 4

/qóm/	/qówm/
/kón/	/kówn/
/tó/	/šówr/
/hól/	/hówl/
/dór/	/dówr/
/józ/	/jówz/

Minimal pairs with /ow/ and /u/:

1.	/tówr/	/túr/
2.	/dówr/	/dúr/
3.	/qówl/	/qúl/
4.	/šówr/	/šúr/
5.	/jówr/	/júr/
6.	/fówt/	/fút/
7.	/sówt/	/sút/

Listen to the set of words. State which two are the same in each set. Assign number 1, 2, or 3.

1	2	3
____	____	____
____	____	____
____	____	____
____	____	____
____	____	____
____	____	____

DIALOG SIX

Vocabulary [9]

bébæxšíd	excuse me
kǽmi	a little
farsí	Persian
ostád	instructor, professor
æræbí	Arabic
mesrí	Eqyptian
almaní	German
iraní	Iranian
torkí	Turkish
ebrí	Hebrew
rusí	Russian
ciní	Chinese
færansé	the French language
færansaví	Frenchman
hendí	Indian
fænlandí	Finnish
danmarkí	Danish
qebrés	Cyprus

---

[9] For additional expressions on languages and nationalities, see Appendix Section A.

Nationalities and Languages

xanóm, šomá koja'í hǽstid?	Excuse me, Miss, where are you from?
mæn amrika'íyæm.	I'm an American.
farsí mídunid?	Do you know Persian?
bǽle, kǽmi farsí mídunæm.	Yes, I know Persian a little.
ostáde šomá koja'íye?	Where is your instructor from?
iraníye.	He's an Iranian.
ostáde æræbí koja'íye?	Where is the Arabic instructor from?
išún mesríye.	She/he is an Egyptian.
ín xanóm æræbí mídune?	Does this lady know Arabic?
næxéyr, æræbí némidune.	No. She doesn't know Arabic.
farsí mídune?	Does she know Persian?
bǽle, farsí xúb mídune.	Yes, she knows Persian well.

Questions:

1. Where is Barbara from?
2. Does she know Persian?
3. Where is Barbara's Persian instructor from?
4. Is the Arabic instructor Iranian or Egyptian?
5. Does Barbara's friend know Persian or Arabic?

PERSONAL PRONOUNS

Following is the list of independent personal pronouns in Persian:

Sg		Pl	
/mǽn/	I	/má/	we
/tó/	thou	/šomá/	you
/ú/	he, she	/išún/	they

A few observations should be made about this set of pronouns:

(1) In the formal style, the plural pronouns are often used for singular referents.
(2) The third person singular distinction is made between human and inanimate (as well as animals). /ú/ 'he, she' is used for human referents, /ún/'it' for objects and animals.
(3) The second person singular, /tó/'thou', is used mostly among close friends, members of the family, and in addressing God.

SUFFIXED PRONOUNS

Suffixed pronouns, unlike independent pronouns, are not words by themselves. They are attached to the preceding word and are considered part of it.

Following is the list of suffixed pronouns.

-æm	-emun
-et, -æt	-etun
-eš, -æš	-ešun

bæradǽre mǽn	bæradǽræm
bæradǽre tó	bæradǽret
bæradǽre ú	bæradǽreš
bæradǽre má	bæradǽremum
bæradǽre šomá	bæradǽretun
bæradǽre išún	bæradǽrešun

Notice that:

(1) All suffixed pronouns begin with a vowel.
(2) Suffixed pronouns do not receive stress.
(3) When a pronoun has to receive stress in a sentence, the independent form of the pronoun is used.

Pattern Drill 6

Practice using the suffixed pronouns.

Step 1

Repeat the following noun phrases using suffixed pronouns, for example:

/hale šomá/   change it into: /háletun/

    1. /sa'æte mæn/
    2. /farsíye má/
    3. /dúste u/
    4. /bæradǽre išún/
    5. /xanóme išún/

Step 2

Substitute the appropriate form of the suffixed pronouns for the independent pronouns in the sentences.

    1. /sa'æte mæn rúye míze/
    2. /ostáde farsíye má iraníye/
    3. /ketábe farsíye dúste u kojást?/
    4. /mænzéle išún næzkíke danešgást/
    5. /keláse u xéyli jalébe/

. (Not on the tape)
6. /kífe šomá siyáhe/
7. /ésme u Minast/
8. /bæradǽre Miná danešjúst/
9. /dúste mǽn almaní míxune/
10. /keláse almaníye išun tú ín saxtemúne/

SUBJECT-VERB AGREEMENT

In Persian, the agreement between the subject and the verb (in person and number) is marked in the form of the verb ending. Consider the following examples:

/mǽn danešjú hǽstæm/	I am a student.
/má danešjú hæstim/	We are students.
/šomá danešjú hæstid/	You are students.

The verb endings are as follows:

	Sg	Pl
1. I	-æm	-im
2. you	-i	-id
3. he/she/it	-e	-ænd

These endings are suffixed to all verb stems, past and present, with one exception. The third person singular of the past stem takes no ending, e.g.,

/ostáde æræbí mesrí búd/	The Arabic instructor was an Egyptian.

(/búd/ is the past stem of 'to be')

The conjugation of the past stem for all persons is:

/búdæm/	I was
/búdi/	you were
/búd/	he, she, it was
/búdim/	we were
/búdid/	you were
/búdænd/	they were

26

/hǽst/, the present stem of 'to be,' takes the same
inflectional endings except for the third person singular
where one of the three variants, /-e, -st, -æst/, is usually
used.

Pattern Drill 7

Substitute the following expressions for the noun phrases
in the pattern and make the necessary changes.

Pattern:

/mǽn kǽmi farsí mídunæm/   I know a little Persian.

1. šomá   6. tó
2. aqáye Hill   7. mæn-o-šomá
3. má   8. mæn
4. xanóm Walsh   9. ín aqá
5. išún

The Postposition /-ra/ and its variants

When the direct object is definite, the postposition /o/ is
used to mark the object (/o/ is used after a consonant), e.g.:

mǽn išúno míšnasæm   I know her.

Pattern Drill 8

Listen and repeat:

mǽn pærvízo xúb míšnasæm

Substitute:

/to/   /išún/
/u/   /Barbara/
/má/   /ostáde má/
/šomá/

27

Notice that the variant /ro/ or /ra/ is used after a vowel:

mǽn ún aqáro mīšnasæm   I know that gentleman.

or

mǽn ún aqára mǐšnasæm

Pattern: mǽn mináro mǐšnasæm

Substitute:

Sará	Miná	Farzané	Holakú
Royá	Ferešté	Haydé	

DIALOG SEVEN

Vocabulary

rǽng	color
pærcǽm	flag
siyáh	black
sefíd	white
sǽbz	green
sórx, qerméz	red
abí	blue
zǽrd	yellow
qæhve'í	brown
xakestærí	grey
narenjí	orange
bænǽfš	purple
surætí	pink
noqre'í	silver
tæla'í	golden
kerém (rǽng)	cream
rowšǽn	light, bright

| sír, tíre | dark |
| surme'í | dark blue |

Colors

ín cíye?	What is this?
ín pærcǽme.	This is a flag.
ín pærcǽme iráne?	Is this the flag of Iran?
bǽle, pærcǽme iráne.	Yes, it is the flag of Iran.
pærcǽme irán cerængíye?	What color is the flag of Iran?
sǽbzo sefído sórxe	It is green, white and red.
ún pærcǽme amrikást?	Is that the flag of the U.S.?
bǽle.	Yes.
pærcǽme amriká cerængíye?	What color is the flag of the U.S.?
abíyo sefído sórxe	It is blue, white and red.

Translate into Persian (not recorded).

1. Is this the flag of Iran?
2. Is that the flag of the U.S.?
3. What color is the flag of Iran?
4. Is the flag of the U.S. blue, white and red?
5. What color is the flag of Iran?
6. Is the flag of Canada white and red?
7. What color is the flag of France?

PRONUNCIATION

Syllable Structure

A syllable is a small unit of speech which consists of consonant(s) and a vowel with stress falling on the vowel. A word in Persian may have as many syllables as it has vowels, e.g.

/má/	we	(1 vowel, 1 syllable)
/væ lí/	but	(2 vowels, 2 syllables)
/da neš gáh/	university	(3 vowels, 3 syllables)
/be sæ la mæt/	good-bye	(4 vowels, 4 syllables)

Type	Example	
CV	/bá/	with
CVC	/báz/	open
CVCC	/níst/	is not

(C stands for consonant and V for vowel.)

Word Stress

A		B	
/gúya/	perhaps	/guyá/	telling
/væli/	but	/vælí/	guardian
/rúzi/	a day	/ruzí/	daily bread
/ketábi/	a book	/ketabí/	bookish
/máhi/	a month	/mahí/	fish

Each pair of the expressions contains the same sequence of sound segments, yet you hear a difference between the two. The difference lies in the degree of "stress" which is given to a given syllable. In all words listed under B, the final syllable receives more emphasis than others. This is not so in words listed under A, where the final syllable is pronounced with a weaker stress.

Pronunciation Drill 5

How many syllables do you identify in the following words? Write the number in the blank space.

1. _____   6. _____

2. _____   7. _____

3. _____   8. _____

4. _____   9. _____

5. _____   10. _____

Pronunciation Drill 6

Underline the stressed syllable.

1. motšækéræm   7. eynǽk

2. bébæxšid   8. xéyli

3. némidunæm   9. vǽli

4. amrika'í   10. ketábi

5. danešgáh   11. tæxtesiyáh

6. dæstmal   12. bǽle

DIALOG EIGHT

Vocabulary

emrúz   today

færdá   tomorrow

pæsfærdá   the day after tomorrow

dirúz	yesterday
šæmbé	Saturday
yek-šæmbé	Sunday
dó-šæmbé	Monday
se-šæmbé	Tuesday
car-šæmbé	Wednesday
pænj-šæmbé	Thursday
jom'é	Friday

Numerals

yazdǽh	11	šunzdǽh	16
dævazdǽh	12	hevdǽh	17
sizdǽh	13	hijdǽh	18
cardǽh	14	nuzdǽh	19
punzdǽh	15	bíst	20

Days of the Week

pærvíz emrúz cænd šæmbǽ:st?	Parviz, what day is it today?
dó šæmbǽ:st.	It is Monday.
færdá cænd šæmbǽ:st?	What day is it tomorrow?
se šæmbǽ:st.	It is Tuesday.
dirúz yekšæmbé búd?	Was it Sunday yesterday?

33

bæle, yekšæmbé búd.		Yes, it was Sunday.	
yekšæmbé danešgáh tæ'tıl búd?		Was the university closed on Sunday?	
bæle, yekšæmbé danešgáh tæ'tıl búd.		Yes. the university was closed on Sunday.	

THE SUFFIX /ÓM/

Ordinal numbers are formed by adding the suffix /om/ to the cardinal numbers.

yék	yekóm	bíst	bistóm
dó	dovvóm	bistoyék	bistoyekóm
sé	sevvóm	bistodó	bistodovvóm
yazdæh	yazdæhóm	bistosé	bistosevvóm
dævazdæh	dævazdæhóm	bistonóh	bistonohóm
sizdæh	sizdæhóm	sí	siyóm
cardæh	cardæhóm	cél	celóm
		pænjáh	pænjahóm

Note that:

(1) The suffix /om/ receives stress.

(2) The ordinal /ævvæl/ 'first' is often used for yekóm.

(3) In compound numerals, the greater number is expressed first, and the lesser followed by the conjunction /o/ as in:

/bíst-o-pænjóm/	25th
/síyo hæftóm/	37th
/cél-o-nohóm/	49th

(4) The ordinal numbers are used in expressing dates:

/emrúz bistóme/
/færdá bísto yekóme/
/pæsfærdá bísto dovvóme/

34

Pattern Drill 9

Give complete answers to the questions.

English translation of the questions:

1. What day is it today?
   Monday.

2. What day will it be tomorrow?
   Tuesday.

3. What day will it be the day after tomorrow?
   Wednesday.

4. What day was it yesterday?
   Sunday.

5. What date is it today?
   12th.

6. What day was it yesterday?
   11th.

Pattern Drill 10

Give complete answers to the questions, using the cues.

English translation of the questions:

1. What color is the flag of Iran?
   Green, white and red.

2. What color is the flag of the U.S.?
   Blue, white and red.

3. What color is the flag of France?
   Blue, white and red.

4. What color is the flag of Canada?
   White and red.

5. What color is the flag of Egpyt?
   Red, white and black.

LONG VS. SHORT FORMS OF 'TO BE'

Compare the following pairs of sentences which contain different forms of 'to be'.

You are a professor.

You are American.

Nader and Parviz are Iranian.

I am a student.

Aside from the present stem /hǽst/ which takes the verb ending, there is a set of related short forms of 'to be'. Compare the short form of 'to be'.

/hǽtæm/	-æm
/hæsti/	-i
/æşt, -e, -st/	-e
/hǽstim/	-im
/hǽstid/	-id
/hæstænd/	-ænd

Pattern Drill 11

Convert the following sentences, using the appropriate short form of the verb 'to be'.

šomá ostád hǽstid

You are a professor.

šomá ostádid

36

TITLES OF ADDRESS

/xanóm/ 'Miss', 'Mrs.' is used both with the first and the family names of the female. The title usually follows the first name, e.g., /pærvín xanóm/, but precedes the family name:

/xanóme rád/	Mrs. Rad
/xanóme pæríye rád/	Mrs. Pari Rad

/xanóm/ may also be used without mentioning the name.

/sælám xanóm/	Hello, Miss (Mrs.)
/xanóm háletun cetówre?/	How are you, lady?

The title /dušîzé/ is used for unmarried young girls:

/dušîzé mæhíne rád/	Miss Mahin Rad
/dušîzé rád/	Miss Rad

/aqá/ 'Mr.' usually follows the first name, e.g., /æhmæd aqá/, but precedes the family name:

/aqáye æhmæde rád/	Mr. Ahmad Rad

SELF-TEST 2

Listening Comprehension

Listen to the following words. State whether the vowel sounds of the words in each pair are the SAME or DIFFERENT.

	SAME	DIFFERENT		SAME	DIFFERENT
1.	_____	_____	6.	_____	_____
2.	_____	_____	7.	_____	_____
3.	_____	_____	8.	_____	_____
4.	_____	_____	9.	_____	_____
5.	_____	_____	10.	_____	_____

Listen to the following words. Determine whether you are identifying a pure vowel or a diphthong in each word. Write V for vowel and D for diphthong in the blank spaces.

1.	_____		10.	_____
2.	_____		11.	_____
3.	_____		12.	_____
4.	_____		13.	_____
5.	_____		14.	_____
6.	_____		15.	_____
7.	_____		16.	_____
8.	_____		17.	_____
9.	_____		18.	_____

In the spaces provided, write the English translation of what you hear on the tape during the pause given.

1. _____

2. _____

3. _____

4. _____

5. _____

6. _____

7. _____

8. _____

9. _____

10. _____

11. _____

12. _____

13. _____

14. _____

15. _____

16. _____

17. _____

18. _____

19. _____

20. _____

21. _____

_____

_____

_____

Vocabulary

1	A	B	C	D
2	A	B	C	D
3	A	B	C	D
4	A	B	C	D
5	A	B	C	D
6	A	B	C	D
7	A	B	C	D
8	A	B	C	D
9	A	B	C	D
10	A	B	C	D

11	A	B	C	D
12	A	B	C	D
13	A	B	C	D
14	A	B	C	D
15	A	B	C	D
16	A	B	C	D
17	A	B	C	D
18	A	B	C	D
19	A	B	C	D
20	A	B	C	D

DIALOG NINE

Vocabulary

rú	on
næzdík	near
tæxte siyáh	blackboard
mænzél	home
æz	from, of
saxtemán	building
otáq	room
ketabxuné	library

Where Is It?

pærvíz ketábet kojást?	Parviz, where is your book?
ketábæm rúye míze.	My book is on the desk.
dæftǽret kojást?	Where's your notebook?
dæftǽræm injást.	My notebook is here.
sændælíye tó næzdíke dǽre?	Is your chair near the door?
næxéyr, næzdíke tæxte siyást.	No, it's near the blackboard.
keláse farsí tú ín saxtemúne?	Is the Persian class in this building?

41

bǽle, tú ín saxtemúne.	Yes, it is in this building.
kelåse æræbí hǽm tú ín saxtemúne?	Is the Arabic class also in this building?
bǽle, tú otáqe sædobíste.	Yes, it is in room 120.
ketabxúne kojást?	Where is the library?
næzdíke resturáne danešgást.	It is near the university restaurant.
mænzéle šomá næzdíke danešgást?	Is your house near the university?
næxéyr, æz danešgáh dúre.	No, it is far from it.

PRONUNCIATION (Consonants)

Most Persian consonants, including those represented in the English spelling by /b,d,t,f,v,j,k,l,m,n,z,p,s/, are close enough to their English counterparts to make a description and provision of systematic practice of them unnecessary here.

A few Persian consonants, however, present problems to speakers of (American) English. This is partly because the sounds do not occur in English. American students are likely to substitute the closest English sounds of their own system for the Persian sounds, for instance, /x/ is often substituted by /k/ by speakers of English. Thus, /xár/ 'thorn' may be pronounced /kár/ 'work' which, of course, is a different word with a different meaning.

The following explanations and drills are meant to help the student overcome problems of this nature.

42

Persian consonants with no English counterparts:

The Consonant /x/

   In pronouncing this sound, the back of the tongue is placed against the velum, and the airstream passes the tongue and the velum. The articulation of /x/ is almost the same as /k/, except that the point of articulation is slightly farther back in the mouth.

Pronunciation Drill 7

/xǽm/	/kǽm/
/xórd/	/kórd/
/xám/	/kám/
/xardár/	/kardár/
/taríx/	/tarík/

   The following word list contrasts /x/ and /k/ sounds. Repeat the words, concentrating on the initial sound of each word.

/kǽm/	/xǽm/
/kórd/	/xórd/
/kám/	/xám/
/kardár/	/xardár/
/tarík/	/taríx/

The Consonant /q/

   In pronouncing the stop variety /q/, the back of the tongue should press the soft palate and uvula. The airstream stops momentarily.

Pronunciation Drill 8

qælǽm	báq
dæqiqé	baqbán
qówm	hoqúq
aqá	bærq
æráq	tæbæqé
qaheré	qurí

43

Pronounce the Persian equivalent of the following expressions. (They all contain the consonant /q/.)

1. pen	6. Cairo
2. teapot	7. room
3. minute	8. red
4. Mr.	9. brown
5. electricity	10. gardener

Pronounce the Persian equivalent of the following expressions that contain the consonant /x/.

1. hard	7. Mrs. Lady
2. blackboard	8. foreigner
3. building	9. sister
4. library	10. grey
5. history	11. red
6. home economics	12. excuse me

DIALOG TEN
(Fields of Study) 10

Vocabulary

míxunid	you study
sǽxt	difficult
asún	easy
jaléb	interesting

---

10 For additional expressions on Fields of Study see Appendix Section A.

taríx	history
zæban-šenasí	linguistics
ketab-darí	library science
fizɪk	physics
šɪmí	chemistry
mærdom-šenasí	anthropology
hæva-šenasí	meteorology
xane-darí	home economics
dæftær-darí	bookkeeping

bébæxšɪd aqá, šomá danešjú hæstid?	Excuse me, Sir, are you a student?
bǽle, mæn danešjú hæstæm.	Yes, I'm a student.
cí míxunid?	What are you studying?
taríxo farsí míxunæm.	I'm studying history and Persian.
dústetun cí míxune?	What does your friend study?
kudúm dústæm?	Which one?
dúste iranítun aqáye færšád.	Your Iranian friend, Mr. Farshad.
išún zæban-šenasí míxune.	He's studying linguistics.
xanómešun cí míxune?	What does his wife study?
ketabdarí míxune.	She's studying library science.

45

ketabdarí sǽxte, ya asúne?	Is the library science hard or easy?
ketabdarí sǽxt níst, xéyli jalébe.	The library science is not hard; it's interesting.

Listen to the conversation between Pari and Nader. After it you will hear a few questions. Try to give answers to the questions in Persian.

Questions:

1. Nadér danešjúst?

2. Nadér cí míxune?

3. aqáye Faršád cí míxune?

4. aqáye Faršad dúste Nadére

5. xanóme aqáye Faršad ketabdarí míxune yá zæban šenasí?

THE CONNECTIVE /e/

Listen to the following noun phrases, paying particular attention to the nouns and their modifiers.

1.	dúst-e-má	our friend
2.	yazdǽh-e-sób	11:00 a.m.
3.	ostád-e-æræbí	the Arabic professor
4.	danešjú-ye-iraní	the Iranian student
5.	dǽrs-e-caróm	the fourth lesson
6.	yék-e-bǽ'd æz zóhr	1:00 p.m.
7.	aqá-ye-Tehrani	Mr. Tehrani

46

8. aqá-ye Nader-e-Tehrani   Mr. Nader Tehrani

9. qǽlæm-e- qermëz   the red pen

10. kót-e- qæhve'í   the brown coat

11. otáq-e- kucík   the small room

12. hævá-ye- gǽrm   the warm weather

A noun may be modified with more than one modifier, e.g.:

dúste iraníye má   Our Iranian friend

ostáde æræbíye danešgáh   The Arabic professor of the
                              university

danešjúye jæváne iraní   The young Iranian student

Pattern Drill 12 (Expansion of the noun phrase)

Repeat the following sentences in Persian, paying particular attention to the order of modifiers in the noun phrases.

(English translation of recorded Persian sentences)

1. Dr. Young is a professor.
   Dr. Young is a professor of Persian.
   Dr. Young is a professor of the Persian language.

2. Sara is a typist.
   Sara is a typist at the library.
   Sara is a typist at the university library.

3. Farzaneh is a librarian.
   Farzaneh is a librarian at the university.
   Farzaneh is a librarian at Columbia University.

THE NEGATIVE OF 'TO BE'

The negative stem of the verb 'to be' is /níst/ to which the inflectional verb endings could be suffixed. The negative paradigm of 'to be' may be listed as:

nístæm	I am not	nístim	we are not
nísti	you are not (Sg)	nístid	you are not
níst	he, she, it is not	nístænd	they are not

The third person singular takes no ending.

Pattern Drill 13 (The negative of 'to be')

Step 1

Listen to the following affirmative statements.

(English translation of recorded Persian statements)

1. I am an American.

2. You are a student.

3. This lady is an Egyptian.

4. We were at the university yesterday.

5. You were at the library at 10:00.

6. Robert was feeling fine yesterday.

7. Our house is near the university.

8. The restaurant is far from here.

9. The library is closed tomorrow.

10. Today is the 20th.

Step 2

Listen to each affirmative statement. Then repeat the statement, using the negative form of the verbs.

Step 3

Translate the sentences given below into Persian.

1. The library is not closed on Saturday.

2. My friend's house is not far from the university.

3. The chemistry class is not in this building.

4. Persian is not difficult.

5. Chinese is not easy.

Step 4

Change the following sentences into the negative.

1. /ún dæstmále/
2. /hále išún xúbe/
3. /ésme ín aqá pærvíze/
4. /ésme ún xanóm barbarást/
5. /ostáde æræbí mesríye/
6. /dúste mæn danešjúst/
7. /ín xanóm amrika'íye/
8. /halá sa'æt cár-o-níme/
9. /be sa'æte šomá car-o-níme/
10. /dúste má danešjúst/
11. /má iraní hæstim/
12. /šomá engelisí hæstid/

DIALOG ELEVEN
(Whose Is It?)

Vocabulary

kelíd	key
mál	property
šuné	comb
dæstkeš	gloves
ruznamé	newspaper
mæjællé	magazine
namé	letter

ín cíye?	What is this?
ún kelíde.	This is a key.
ín kelíd mále kíye?	Whose key is this?
mále šomást.	It's yours.
kelíde mǽn kojást?	Where is my key?
rúye míze.	It's on the table.
iná cíyænd?	What are these?
uná medádænd.	They're pencils.
iná medadáye kíyænd?	Whose pencils are these?

uná medadáye šománd.	They're yours.
medadáye mǽn kojánd?	Where are my pencils?
unjánd.	They're over there.
ín šunehá mále kíyænd?	Whose combs are these?
mále mǽnænd.	They are mine.
šuneháye šomá cerǽngænd?	What color are your combs?
siyáhænd.	They're green.
ín qælǽme šomást?	Is this your pen?
bǽle, mále mǽne.	Yes, it's mine.

PRONUNCIATION (The glottal stop, /'/, /hæmzé/)

In pronouncing this sound the vocal cords are brought together to block the flow of the airstream and are opened suddenly to release the built-up pressure. The resulting sound is called the glottal stop.

There are pairs of words in Persian which are different because of the presence or absence of the glottal stop, e.g.:

/bædǽn/	body	vs.	/bæ'dǽn/	later on
/sǽd/	hundred	vs.	/sǽ'd/	fortunate
/šǽm/	smelling	vs.	/šǽm'/	candle

Pronunciation Drill 9

Listen to the following words that contain the glottal stop.

bǽ'd	tæ'tíl	ro'yá ,
bæ'd ,æz zóhr	jom'é	qæra'æt
bæ'ǰæn	rób'	so'ál
sa'æt	'æræbí	tæ'xír
	'ebrí	

52

The glottal stop is usually omitted in rapid informal spoken Persian. The sound may occur in all positions. Its occurrence in initial position is automatic and predictable. Therefore, it has been disregarded in the transcription system used in this book. In other positions, medial and final, although the sound may disappear in pronunciation, the symbol /'/ has been used to represent the glottal stop.

DIALOG TWELVE
(Review)

Vocabulary

zæbán	language, tongue
xarejí	foreign
næzǽr	view, opinion
be næzǽre šomá	in your opinion
lahjé	dialect
ræsmí	official
zæbáne madærí	mother tongue

aqáye Farshad šomá cǽnd ta ostáde engelisí darid?	Mr. Farshad, how many English professors do you have?
má dó ta ostáde engelisí darim.	We have two professors.
ostadátun zæbáne xarejí hæm mídunænd?	Do your professors know foreign languages also?
bæle, yekíšun farsíyo espanoyolí mídune, yekíšun hæm æræbíyo almaní.	Yes, one of them knows Persian and Spanish, and one knows Arabic and German.

šomá cǽnd ta zæbúne xarejí mídunid?	How many foreign languages do you know?
mǽn engelisíyo æræbí mídunæm.	I know English and Arabic.
benæzǽre šomá engelisí sǽxte ya asúne?	In your opinion is English difficult or easy?
benæzǽre mæn engelisí sǽxt níst.	In my opinion English is not difficult.
æræbí cetówr?	How about Arabic?
æræbí æz ̦ engelisí sǽxt-tære.	Arabic is more difficult than English.

COMPARATIVE DEGREE OF ADJECTIVES

The comparative is formed by adding the suffix /tær/ to adjectives:

/bozórg/	/bozorgtær/
/kucík/	/kuciktær/
/bǽd/	/bædtær/
/xúb/	/behtær/
/gǽrm/	/gærmtær/
/særd/	/særdtæ̦r/
/jaléb/	/jalebtæ̦r/
/jæván/	/jævantær/

Note that:

(1) The stress always falls on the suffix /tǽr/.
(2) The preposition /æz/ corresponds to the English 'than'.
(3) /behtǽr/ 'better' is more common than the regular comparative /xubtǽr/.

Pattern Drill 14 (Part A)

Combine each pair of sentences using the comparative degree of adjectives.

Example:

a. /farsí asúne/
b. /engelisí xéyli asúne/
/engelisí æz farsí asuntǽre/

1. a. /almaní sǽxte/
   b. /rusí xéyli sǽxte/

2. a. /engelisí asúne/
   b. /farsí xéyli asúne/

3. a. /keláse má kucıke/
   b. /keláse torkí xéyli kucıke/

4. a. /emrúz gǽrme/
   b. /dirúz xéyli gǽrm búd/

POSSESSION

Possession may be expressed by either "ezafé construction" or the use of /mál/ 'property' as in the examples:

/ín, ketábe šomást/   This is your book.

/ín ketáb, mále šomást/   This book is yours.

Pattern Drill 14 (Part B)

Repeat the following sentences using the expression /mál/.

1. /ún, medáde šomást/   5. /ín cǽtre šomást?/
2. /ún kífe nadére/   6. /ín cǽtre bæradǽre šomást?/
3. /ín, ruznaméye pævíze/   7. /ín qælǽme táme?/
4. /ún eynǽke pærvíne/   8. /ín qælǽme dúste táme?/

THE NEGATIVE FORMS OF VERBS

Aside from the verb 'to be', which has the negative stem /níst/ 'is not', the negative form of all other verbs is accompanied by the negative prefix /næ/ or its variant /ne/. The negative prefix /næ/ is used whenever there is no other verb prefix.

dárim	we have	:	nǽdarim	we don't have
búd	it was	:	nǽbud	it was not

/ne/ precedes the verb form beginning with the prefix /mi/:

mídunid	you know	:	némidunid	you don't know
mígoft	he would say	:	némigoft	he wouldn't say

Pattern Drill 15 (The negative forms of verbs)

Substitute the following subject pronouns in the pattern.

Pattern: mæn æræbi nemidunæm

/tó/	/má/	/íšún/
/ú/	/šomá/	/mǽn/

SELF-TEST 3

Listening Comprehension

a. Listen to the polysyllabic words you hear on the tape. Underline the stressed syllable and indicate the number of syllables. Write the number in the blank spaces.

1. danešju _____   3. amrika _____

2. mišenasid _____   4. almani _____

5. engelisitun ____   8. zæbanšenasi ____

6. kucik ____   9. zæbane xareji ____

7. xaharasun ____   10. ruznameha ____

b. True/False Questions

11. ____   16. ____

12. ____   17. ____

13. ____   18. ____

14. ____   19. ____

15. ____   20. ____

Vocabulary

33. _____ _____

34. _____ _____

35. _____ _____

36. _____ _____

37. _____ _____

38. _____ _____

Oral Translation

39. _____   40. _____   41. _____   42. _____

43. _____   44. _____   45. _____   46. _____

47. _____   48. _____   49. _____   50. _____

DIALOG THIRTEEN
(Family Relationships I)

Vocabulary

bæradǽr	brother
bozórg	big
kucík	small
sál	year
dæbestán	elementary school
dæbirestán	high school
xahǽr	sister
šowhǽr	husband
ezdeváj kærdǽn	to get married

bébæxšid xanóm, šomá cǽnd bæradǽr dárid?	Excuse me, Miss, how many brothers do you have?
mǽn yék bæradǽr dáræm.	I have one brother.
ésme bæradǽretun cíye?	What's the name of your brother?
ésmeš mæs'úde.	His name is Mas'ud.
mæs'úd æz šomá bozorgtǽre, ya kuciktǽre?	Is Mas'ud older or younger than you are?
sé sál æz mǽn kuciktǽre.	He's three years younger than I am.

bæradæretun dæbestán míre?	Does your brother go to the elementary school?
næxéyr, dæbirestán míre, keláse nohóme.	No. He goes to the high school. He's in the ninth grade.
šomá xahǽr hǽm dárid?	Do you also have any sisters?
bǽle, dó xahǽr dáræm.	Yes, I have two sisters.
xahærátun æz šomá kucik-tǽrænd?	Are your sisters younger than you are?
æz mæn bozorgtærænd.	No. They are older than I am.
xahærátun cekár míkonænd?	What do your sisters do?
yék xahǽræm danešjúst, yéki hæm ba šowhæreš dær irán zendegi míkone.	One of my sisters is a student, the other lives with her husband in Iran.

(Translation of recorded questions)

1. How many brothers does Pari have?
2. What is the name of her brother?
3. Is Mas'ud older or younger than Pari?
4. How many years is Pari older than Mas'ud?
5. Does Mas'ud go to school?
6. How many sisters does Pari have?
7. Is Pari older or younger than her sisters?
8. In one of her sisters a student?
9. Does one of her sisters live in Iran?

PRONUNCIATION (Consonants with close counterparts in English)

In the category of "close substitute" sounds, we may point out a few consonants including /l/, /r/, and /h/. These consonants are not completely new sounds to speakers of English. The

Persian /l/ is similar to the English /l/ in syllable-initial positions, e.g.:

lǽb	lip
lebás	clothing
lǽndǽn	London

In Persian, regardless of its position, /l/ is pronounced the same way. The variety of the English /l/ which occurs in syllable-final or pre-consonantal (e.g., mail, halt, etc.) does not appear in Persian.

Pronunciation Drill 10

lebás	sǽndǽlí
lóft	dǽstmál
lǽndǽn	famíl
qǽlǽm	mǽnzél
kelíd	so'ál

DIALOG FOURTEEN
(Family Relationships II)

Vocabulary

madǽr	mother
da'í	uncle
yǽ'ǽní	means
motǽrjém	translator

sefarǽt	embassy
xalé	aunt
æmmú	uncle
æmmé	aunt
pedǽr bozórg	grandfather
madǽr bozórg	grandmother
pesǽr da'í	cousin
doxtǽr da'í	niece

xanóm walš, pedǽr-o-madǽretun kojá zendegi míkonænd?	Miss Walsh, where do your parents live?
dær Tehrán zendegi míkonænd.	They live in Tehran.
da'ítun kojá zendegi míkone?	Where does your uncle live?
bébæxšid, da'í yæ'æní ci?	Excuse me, what does 'da'i' mean?
da'í yæ'æni bærdǽre madǽr.	'da'i' means mother's brother.
da'ím dær Tehrán zendegí míkone.	My uncle lives in Tehran.
dær Tehrán cekár míkone?	What does he do in Tehran?
motærjéme.	He is a translator.
da'ítun cǽnd zæbán mídune?	How many languages does your uncle know?

cár ta zæbán mídune, engelisí, torkí, almaní, farsí.	He knows four languages, English, Turkish, German and Persian.
šomá xalé hæm dárid?	Do you also have aunts?
bébæxšid, xalé yæ'æní ci?	Excuse me, what does 'xale' mean?
xalé yæ'æní xáhre madǽr.	'xale' means mother's sister.
bǽle, mæn yék xalé hæm dáræm.	Yes, I have also one aunt.

THE PLURAL SUFFIXES (/-há/, /-á/)

A singular noun may form its plural by one of the plural suffixes. The most common plural suffix in the informal style is /-á/, which has the variant /-há/. The former is used after consonants and the latter after vowels:

Post-consonant:

Sg		Pl	
/kelás/	class	/kelasá/	classes
/ostád/	instructor	/ostadá/	instructors

Post-vowel:

/já/	place	/jahá/	places
/ruznamé/	paper	/ruznamehá/	papers

63

Pattern Drill 16

Repeat the following sentences, changing the subject and the verbs into the plural:

Example:

/bæradǽræm dæbestán míre/ : /bæradǽram dæbestán mírænd/

1.

2.

3.

4.

5.

COMPLEMENTS OF THE VERB 'TO BE'

A variety of structures may precede the verb 'to be' as its complement. Some of these structures are pointed out in the examples:

(1) /ésme ín áqa pærvíze/ The name of this gentleman is Parviz.

(2) /hále pærvíz xúbe/ He is fine.

(3) /ketábæm rúye míze/ My book is on the desk.

(4) /færdá bisto-caróme/ Tomorrow is the twenty-fourth.

In sentence (1), the complement of 'be' is a noun phrase. In sentence (2), 'be' is preceded by an adjective. In sentence (3), the complement of 'be' is a prepositional phrase. In sentence (4), /bist-o-caróm/ 'the twenty-fourth' is a noun phrase functioning as an adverb of time.

Pattern Drill 17

Make original sentences using the following phrases as the complement of the verb 'to be'. Use the verb 'to be' affirmatively. Examples:

the complement   /zíre sændælí/

the sentence   /kífe ún xanóm zíre sændælíye/

Phrases to be used as complement:

1. /aqáye nadére tehraní/

2. /xanóme pæríye qæríb/

3. /xúb/

4. /næzdíke keláse farsí/

5. /tæ'tíl/

6. /kojá/

7. /kí/

8. /caršæmbé, bist-o-pænjóm/

9. /jom'e nohóme desámr/

10. /sa'æte dævazhæh-o-ním/

Translate into Persian:

1. Your handkerchief is on my desk.

2. The eraser is under the chair.

3. Is your friend a student?

4. Where is your house?

5. Is it near the university?

Underline the complements of the verb 'to be' in the
following sentences.

1. /færdá danešgáh tæ'tıl níst/

2. /lebasáš rúye míze mǽn níst, rúye sændælíye/

3. /mænzéle má æz injá kǽmi dúre/

4. /keláse farsí tú in santemún níst, tú saxtemúne
   ketebxunǽst/

5. /Mina se sál æz bæradǽre mǽn bozogtǽre/

DIALOG FIFTEEN
(People and Occupations) 11

Vocabulary

karmǽnd	employee
bánk	bank
mærkǽz	center
mærkæzí	central
pesǽr	son, boy
æfsǽr	officer
nirú	force
pæræstár	nurse
hesabdár	accountant
monší	secretary
dæbír	high school teacher
ruzname-nevís	journalist
nevisændé	writer

šomá aqáye ironíyo mísnasid?	Do you know Mr. Irani?
bǽle, išún-o xúb mísnasæm, dúste pedæræme.	Yes, I know him well. He is my father's friend.

11 See Appendix Section A for more occupations.

aqáye iraní cekár mıkone?	What does Mr. Irani do?
karmǽnde bánke.	He is an employee of the bank.
kudúm bánk?	Which bank?
išún karmǽnde bánke mærkæzíye iráne.	He is the employee of the Central Bank of Iran.
pesǽre aqáye iraní cekár mıkone?	What does his son do?
dær šerkǽte nǽft kár mıkone, mohændése.	He works for the Oil Company. He is an engineer.
ín aqá cekarǽ:st?	What does this gentleman do?
išún æfsǽre, æfsǽre nirúye hæva'íye.	He is an officer. He is a navy officer.
ún xanóm cekár mıkone?	What does that lady do?
mašín nevíse, tu ketab-xunéye danešgáh kar mıkone.	She is a typist. She works at the university library.
šowhæreš cekár mıkone?	What does her husband do?
dæbíre dæbiretáne.	He is a high school teacher.

PRONUNCIATION (The consonant /h/)

Like its counterpart in English, /h/ is a glottal sound. In its articulation, the airstream passes through the glottis with friction.

This sound is similar to its English counterpart, except that you will have to learn to pronounce it in medial and final position as well.

Pronunciation Drill 11

Listen to the following words that contain the consonant /h/.

a. Initial /h/	b. Medial /h/	c. Final /h/
/hævá/	/šæhr/	/danešgáh/
/hæftád/	/pǽhn/	/yazdǽh/
/hæštád/	/zǽhr/	/gorúh/
/hezár/	/fǽhm/	/koláh/
/hæmišé/	/nǽhv/	/máh/

DIALOG SIXTEEN
(Talking About the Weather) [12]

Vocabulary

dišǽb	last night
bǽrf	snow
xéyli	a lot
radiyó	radio
aftabí	sunny
zemestún	winter
gáhi	occasionally
tabestún	summer
gǽrm	warm

---

[12] Additional expressions on weather are given in Appendix Section A.

mærtúb	humid
æbr	cloud
xóšk	dry
molayém	wild
bahár	spring
pa'íz	fall

sælám mæryæm.	Hello, Maryam.
sælam Parviz, hálet xúbe?	Hello, Parviz. Are you feeling fine?
bæd níst, motšækkéræm.	Not bad, thanks.
rastí dišæb bærf umæd?	By the way, did it snow last night?
bæle, xéyli bærf umæd.	Yes, it snowed a lot.
færdá hævá cetówre? færdá hæm bærf míyad?	How's the weather tomorrow? Is it going to snow tomorrow, too?
næxéyr, radíyo góft færdá aftabíye.	No. The radio said it would be sunny tomorrow.
injá zemestún xéyli bærf míyad?	Does it snow a lot here in the winter?
næ, gáhi bærf míyad, væli bištær barún míyad.	No. It occasionally snows, but it rains very often.
tabessún hævá cetówre?	How's the weather in the summer?
kæmi gærme, væli mærtúb níst.	It's a little bit warm, but it's not humid.

70

(Translation of the recorded questions)

1. Does it snow in the winter here?
2. How is the weather in the summer?
3. Is the weather in the spring mild or warm?
4. Is the weather in the summer dry or humid?
5. Does it rain a lot in the fall?
6. How is the weather today?
7. Did it rain last night?
8. Is tomorrow sunny or cloudy?

Pattern Drill 18

You will hear statements about today's weather. Ask questions, using the past tense for the time expression given.

Example:

| You will hear: | /emrúz hævá gǽrme/ |
| You say: | /dirúz hævá gǽrm búd?/ |

VERB STEMS

All verb forms in Persian operate on one of the two stems, i.e., the past verb stem and the present verb stem.[13] A few examples will illustrate the relationship between the two stems:

Past	Present	
/búd/	/hǽst/	to be
/góft/	/-g-/	to say

---

[13] Persian dictionaries usually give the infinitive of the verbs from which only the past stem can be found (by deleting the infinitive marker /-æn/, e.g., /budǽn/ 'to be' to /búd/, the past stem, etc.)

Since the present stem is not predictable from the infinitive (except for the 'regular' verbs), it is usually cited together with the infinitive.

/umǽd/	/-a-/	to come
/xúnd/	/xún/	to study
/dašt/	/dár/	to have
/kóšt/	/kóš/	to kill
/šenáxt/	/šenás/	to know (somebody)
/dunést/	/dún/	to know (something)
/díd/	/bín/	to see
/nešǽst/	/nešín/	to sit
/dád/	/-d/	to give
/nevéšt/	/nevís/	to write

Pattern Drill 19 (Verb stems)

What is the past stem of the following infinitives?

/budǽn/	to be
/goftǽn/	to say
/umædǽn/	to come
/ræftǽn/	to go
/xundǽn/	to study
/daštǽn/	to have

Let's see if you remember the present stem of the same verbs.

Past	Present
/búd/	_____
/góft/	_____
/uméd/	_____
/xúnd/	_____
/dašt/	_____
/kóšt/	_____
/šenáxt/	_____
/dunést/	_____
/díd/	_____
/nešést/	_____
/dád/	_____
/nevéšt/	_____

Pattern Drill 20 (Use of simple present tense for future)

Repeat the following sentences using the simple present tense and the time expression /færda/. Let's begin with the verbs 'to be' and 'to have'. Remember that the present stem of these two verbs does not take the verb prefix /mi-/.

Listen to the example:

mǽn dirúz kelás dáštæm.   mǽn færdá kelás dáræm.

šomá dirúz injá búdid.   šomá færdá injá hǽstid.

73

1. You had history yesterday.

2. Robert had Persian yesterday.

3. Nader and Parviz had English yesterday.

4. You had Arabic yesterday.

5. We had physics and chemistry yesterday.

6. I was home at eight o'clock yesterday.

7. You were home yesterday.

8. Robert was not home yesterday.

Pattern Drill 21 (People and occupations)

Listen to the following short conversations. You will then be asked to answer the questions, using the cues given.

SELF-TEST 4

Listening Comprehension

Listen to the following questions and answers. Each question will be followed by three answers. Circle A, B, or C according to whether the best answer to the question is the first, second or third one heard. Listen to the example:

1	A	B	C
2	A	B	C
3	A	B	C
4	A	B	C
5	A	B	C

6	A	B	C
7	A	B	C
8	A	B	C
9	A	B	C
10	A	B	C

11	A	B	C
12	A	B	C
13	A	B	C
14	A	B	C
15	A	B	C

True-False Questions

1. _____   4. _____

2. _____   5. _____

3. _____   6. _____

Translation

1. _____   11. _____

2. _____   12. _____

3. _____   13. _____

4. _____   14. _____

5. _____   15. _____

6. _____   16. _____

7. _____   17. _____

8. _____   18. _____

9. _____   19. _____

10. _____   20. _____

Vocabulary

1. _____   6. _____

2. _____   7. _____

3. _____   8. _____

4. _____   9. _____

5. _____

DIALOG SEVENTEEN
(Making Requests I and II)

Vocabulary

lotfǽn	please
besyár xúb	all right
báz	open
bæsté	closed
xahéš mıkonæm	I beg to ask
béfærma'id	here you are
mæ'zerǽt míxam	I am sorry
hævapeymá	airplane
hærekæt kærdǽn	to leave
residǽn	to arrive, to get to

mundǽn	to stay
fekr kærdǽn	to think
edaré	office

Making Requests (I)

aqáye vafa'í, lotfæn ketábetun-o báz kónid.	Mr. Vafa'i, please open your book.
besyár xúb.	All right.
halá lotfǽn ketábetun-o bébændid.	Now, please close your book.
besyár xúb.	All right.
aqáye vafa'í, lotfǽn dǽre kelás-o báz kónid.	Mr. Vafa'i, please open the classroom door.
xéyli xúb.	All right.
halá lotfǽn dǽr-o bébændid.	Now, please close the door.
besyár xúb.	All right.
áli, kí dǽr-o bǽst?	Ali, who closed the door?
aqáye vafa'í dǽr-o bǽst.	Mr. Vafa'i closed the door.
halá dǽre kelás báze, yá bǽstǽ:st?	Is the classroom door open or closed?
bǽstǽ:st.	It is closed.
pænjeré báze, yá bǽstǽ:st?	Is the window open or closed?
báze.	It is open.

PRONUNCIATION   (The consonant /r/)

This sound may be trill or flap in Persian.

In pronouncing the trill /r/, the tongue tip strikes the alveolar ridge several times in rapid succession:

/ruznamé/   newspaper

/resalé/   thesis

/karxané/   factory

In pronouncing the flap /r/ the tongue tip quickly strikes the alveolar ridge once (not in succession as for the trill /r/):

/bazár/   marketplace

Pronunciation Drill 12

Listen to the following words that contain the consonant /r/:

a. Initial /r/	b. Medial /r/	c. Final /r/
/ráh/	/emrúz/	/šǽhr/
/rǽng/	/færdá/	/divár/
/rowšǽn/	/dirúz/	/dúr/
/resturán/	/taríx/	/zír/
/rúz/	/iraní/	/bazár/

Making Requests (II)

xanóm téhrani lotfǽn   Mrs. Tehrani, please give me
   dæftǽretun-o be mǽn bédid.   your notebook.

78

béfærma'id.	Here you are.
náder, kí dæftæreš-o be mæn dád?	Nader, who gave her notebook to me?
xanóm tehrani dæftæreš-o be šomá dád.	Mrs. Tehrani gave her notebook to you.
aqáye vafa'í, lotfæn dælæmetun-o be mæn bédid.	Mr. Vaf'ai, please give me your pen.
béfærma'id.	Here you are.
mæn halá ésmetun-o rúye dæftæretun mínevisæm.	Now, I'll write your name on your notebook.
náder šomá hæm ésmetun-o rúye dæftæretun bénevisid.	Nader, you also write your name on your notebook.
besyár xúb.	All right.
aqáye vafa'í, kí ésmeš-o rúye dæftæreš nevešt?	Mr. Vafa'i, who wrote his name on his notebook?
náder ésmeš-o rúye dæftæreš nevešt.	Nader wrote his name on his notebook.
xanóme tehraní lotfæn ín kælæmé-ro béxunid.	Mrs. Tehrani, please read this word.
besyár xúb.	All right.

IMPERATIVE SENTENCES

A. Notice the difference (in verb form) between an affirmative statement and an affirmative command.

/šomá farsí míxunid/	You study Persian.
/farsí béxunid/	Study Persian.

The verb prefix /mi-/ is replaced by /be-/ and the expressed subject /šomá/ 'you' drops in the imperative, but the verb ending is retained.

B. The negative marker /næ-/ replaces the prefix /be-/ as in the example:

> /dær-o bédændid/   Close the door.
>
> /dær-o næbændid/   Don't close the door.

In the polite style, the verb ending /-id/ is used for singular, e.g.:

> /lotfǽn béxunid/   Please read (sg).

No verb ending is used in the familiar singular, which corresponds with the subject pronoun /tó/ 'thou':

> /tó farsí míxuni/   You (sg) study Persian.
>
> /farsí béxun/   Study Persian (sg).

Pattern Drill 22

Step 1.   What is the formal request form of the following verbs?

Step 2.   What is the request form of the same verbs in the informal, familiar style?

Step 3.   Translate into Persian:

1. Please write your name.
2. Go over there.
3. Give me your notebook.
4. Don't open the window.
5. Come to our house at 8:00 tomorrow.

Pattern Drill 23 (Negative Imperative)

Substitute the following words in the pattern.

<u>Pattern</u>:

1. word
2. words
3. letter
4. letters

5. note
6. notes
7. drill
8. drills

FINAL EXAMINATION
(SELF-TEST)

The test items included herein are based on all the materials presented in the course. The result of this test will help you find out how well you have learned Persian so far.

The test is divided into four sections:

(1) listening comprehension;

(2) speaking and listening comprehension;

(3) vocabulary;

(4) grammar and written translation.

Listening Comprehension

You will hear several pairs of expressions. Each pair is pronounced once. Then a short pause will follow during which you check the appropriate column.

	SAME	DIFFERENT		SAME	DIFFERENT
1.	_____	_____	6.	_____	_____
2.	_____	_____	7.	_____	_____
3.	_____	_____	8.	_____	_____
4.	_____	_____	9.	_____	_____
5.	_____	_____	10.	_____	_____

Listen to the sentences. Check the Question column if the sentence is interrogative, or the Statement column if the sentence is a statement.

	QUESTION	STATEMENT		QUESTION	STATEMENT
11.	_____	_____	16.	_____	_____
12.	_____	_____	17.	_____	_____
13.	_____	_____	18.	_____	_____
14.	_____	_____	19.	_____	_____
15.	_____	_____	20.	_____	_____

Listen to the following groups of sentences. In the pause following the three sentence groups, determine which two are the same by checking the appropriate column. Listen to the example:

A. /dirúz sevvóm búd/

B. /dirúz sevvóm búd/

C. /dirúz siyóm búd/

Check A and B because the first two sentences sound the same.

21	A	B	C
22	A	B	C
23	A	B	C
24	A	B	C
25	A	B	C

26	A	B	C
27	A	B	C
28	A	B	C
29	A	B	C
30	A	B	C

31	A	B	C
32	A	B	C
33	A	B	C
34	A	B	C
35	A	B	C

36	A	B	C
37	A	B	C
38	A	B	C
39	A	B	C
40	A	B	C

Listen to the following passages. Each passage will be read twice. After the second reading, the passage is followed by a series of questions. Select the best answer by circling A, B, or C.

41	A	B	C
42	A	B	C
43	A	B	C
44	A	B	C
45	A	B	C
46	A	B	C
47	A	B	C
48	A	B	C
49	A	B	C
50	A	B	C

Speaking and Listening Comprehension

a. Give a complete grammatical answer to each of the following questions.

b. Look at the picture before you answer each question. Relate your answer to the situation you see in each picture.

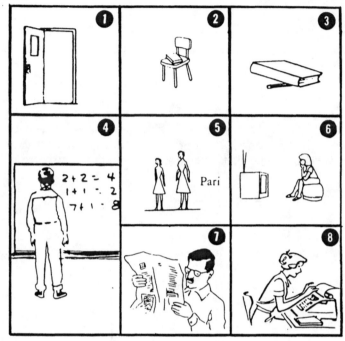

c. Listen to the dialog. Then answer the questions.

Vocabulary

One of the four expressions that you hear on the tape matches the English word listed in your book. Circle A, B, C, or D.

1. engineer	A B C D	4. aunt	A B C D
2. high school	A B C D	5. dialect	A B C D
3. typist	A B C D	6. to stay	A B C D

7. Friday	A B C D	12. cloudy	A B C D
8. to lose	A B C D	13. tomorrow	A B C D
9. a note	A B C D	14. excuse me	A B C D
10. anthropology	A B C D	15. to see	A B C D
11. difficult	A B C D		

Which of the four Persian expressions that you hear on the tape is the opposite of the English word listed in your book? Circle A, B, C, or D.

1. to arrive	A B C D	5. never	A B C D
2. a lot	A B C D	6. far	A B C D
3. displeased	A B C D	7. small	A B C D
4. humid	A B C D	8. black	A B C D

Which of the four expressions you hear on the tape is equivalent to the English word listed in your book?

1. in your opinion	A B C D	5. to think	A B C D
2. afternoon	A B C D	6. light	A B C D
3. to teach	A B C D	7. last year	A B C D
4. a nurse	A B C D	8. grey	A B C D

Stop the tape here and answer the questions in the next section.

Grammar and Translation

Match the Persian verb forms with the English verb forms. Write the corresponding letters in the parentheses.

a. ræft   ( ) he gave

b. umǽdæm   ( ) it was

c. dád   ( ) you are

d. míneveš,tim   ( ) go

e. míbinim   ( ) is

f. búd   ( ) we see

g. dáštænd   ( ) they had

h. hǽstid   ( ) they have

i. bóro   ( ) I open

j. bíya   ( ) please close

k. ǽst   ( ) I came

l. dárænd   ( ) it came, he came

m. baz míkonæm   ( ) he went

n. bédændid   ( ) come!

o. mídunid   ( ) you know

p. baz mıkone   ( ) he opens

q. míbændænd   ( ) we would write, we used to write

r. béxunid   ( ) they close

s. míšnasæm   ( ) please read

t. umǽd   ( ) I know (somebody)

88

Match the present stems of the verbs with the past stems. Write the corresponding letters in the parentheses.

Past Stems

a. umǽd
b. rǽft
c. góft
d. nevéšt
e. dád
f. xórd
g. búd
h. díd
i. nešǽst
j. bǽst

Present Stems

( ) g
( ) d
( ) ro
( ) xor
( ) hæst
( ) bin
( ) nevis
( ) bænd
( ) a
( ) nesin

Translate into English.

1. /ketábe farsí/
2. /míbændæm/
3. /pænjeréye otáq/
4. /báz míkonæm/
5. /cǽtre išún/
6. /kaqǽze dústæm/
7. /míxunæm/
8. /ruznzméye engelisí/
9. /ín kaqǽz/
10. /mínevisæm/

1. _____

2. _____

3. _____

4. _____

5. _____

6. _____

7. _____

8. _____

9. _____

10. _____

1. /mǽn dǽr ín danešgáh farsí míxunæm/
2. /tó dǽr ín kelás farsí míxuni/
3. /ín xanóm engelisí xúb mídune/
4. /ú ostáde taríxe/
5. /ún aqá espanyolí némidune/
6. /šomá išún-o mīšnasid?/
7. /mǽn amrik'í hǽstæm?/
8. /keláse má dirúz tæ'tíl bud?/
9. /šomá ín xanóm-o mīšnasind?/
10. /šomá halá farsí xúb mídunid?/

1. _____

2. _____

3. _____

4. _____

5. _____

6. _____

7. _____

8. _____

9. _____

10. _____

English	Persian
Hello.	sælám 'æléykom.
How are you?	æhvále šæríſ cetówre?
Oh, thank you, I am well. (Lit. as a result of your inquiring after my health)--said ironically, complaining of someone not having inquired after one's health.	ey, æz æhvalposiyáye šomá.
How are you?	cetówri?
I am not in a good mood.	sære hal nístæm.
Are you fine?	hálet xúbe?
Not so bad.	ey, bæd níst.
God bless, what is wrong with you? I hope it is not serious.	xodá bæd næde, enša'ælláh bælá dúre.
I have caught a cold. My body aches.	særmá xordæ:m. tænæm dærd míkone.
How are you today?	emrúz cetówri?
Thanks to God. I am feeling better.	ælhæmdolláh behtæræm.
What is wrong with Robert?	Robert ceše?
He is very busy.	særeš xeyli šulúqe (Lit. Around his head is too crowded)

Leave-taking Expressions

Good-bye. (Lit. God may keep you.)	xodá negæhdár.
Good-bye. (Lit. May your favor increase.)	mærhæméte šomá ziyád.
Good night.	šǽb xóš.
Good luck to you.	bé æmáne xodá.
Have a nice trip.	sæfǽr bexéyr.
to you	'æléykom
I	bændé (Lit. slave)
plural of /hal/ 'condition'	æhvál
honoring	tæšríf
inquiring after one's health	æhvalporsí
in a good mood	sære hál
God willing	enša'ælláh
evil	bælá
far	dúr
to catch a cold	særmá xordæn
body	tǽn
to ache	dærd kærdǽn
thanks to God	ælhæmdolláh

better	behtǽr
crowded	šulúq

Introduction

to introduce	mo'ǽrrefi kǽrdǽn
pleased	xošvǽqt
to know (somebody)	šenaxtǽn
to hear	šǽnidǽn
to speak	sohbǽt kǽrdǽn
in a familiar way	xodemuní
to give	dadǽn
permission	ejazé
to have	daštǽn
old	qǽdimí
each other, together	ba hǽ́m
to become	šodǽn
familiar	ašená
still, yet	hǽnúz
Allow me to introduce myself.	ejazé bédid xódǽmo mo'rrefí konǽm.
I am Parviz Kiani.	bǽndé Parviz kianí.
May I introduce my friend to you?	ejazé bédid dústǽmo be šomá mo'ǽrrefí kónǽm.

93

You don't know Mr. Rad, do you?	mésle ínke aqáye Rado némišnasid?
I don't think I have met him before.	išúno bejá némiyaræm.
I am glad to know you.	æz ašna'í ba šomá xošvǽqtæm.
Excuse me, I didn't catch your name.	bébæxšid, ésmetuno doróst næšænidæm.

Expressions of Courtesy

Please!	béfærma'id. (When offering to someone: to have something to eat, to speak, to take a seat, to enter first, to act, etc.)
Please do come in!	béfærma'id tu.
Why don't you take a seat?	céra némifærma'id?
After you.	avvǽl šomá béfærma'id.
What can I do for you?	cé færmayéšĭ dárid?
It is awfully good of you.	xéyli lótf færmúdid.
You are very kind indeed.	lóft dárid.
Excuse me, sir.	bébæxšid, aqá.
Excuse me.	'ózr míxam.
I am afraid I am wasting your time.	bébæxšid vǽqte šomáro mígiræm..
I am sorry to have troubled you.	bébæxšid æsbábe zæhmǽte šomá šódæm.
No trouble at all.	cé zæhmǽti!

Please! I beg to ask.	xahéš míkonæm.
Please speak more slowly.	xahéš míkonæm kǽmi ahestetǽr sohbǽt kónid.
With pleasure!	cǽšm, becǽšm.
Thanks.	mæmnún.
Thank you.	mæmnúnæm.
Not at all. Don't mention it. That's alright. (Lit. You have the option.)	extiyár dárid.
Don't mention it. (said in answer to someone thanking for an offer)	qabéli nǽdare.
It doesn't matter.	éyb nǽdare.
Doctor	aqáye doktór
(Lit. Mech. Engineer)	aqáye mohændés
Sir. My Lord.	qórban
Your Excellency	jenábe 'alí
Dear mother.	madǽr jún.
Parviz sends you his greetings.	Parviz be šomá sælám míresune.
Remember me to him.	sæláme mǽno be išún béresunid.

Nationalities, Languages and Places

Indian	hendí
Finnish	fænlandí

Danish	danmarkí
Cyprus	qebrés
Israel	esra'íl
Mexico	mekzík
Chili	šilí
Urdu	ordú
Armenian	ærmæní
Vietnam	vietnám
The Philippines	filipín
Sudan	sudán
Morocco	mærakéš

Expressions of Agreement and Disagreement

Yes.	aré.
Of course.	ælbǽte.
Just so. You are right.	doróste.
Quite so. You are in the right.	hǽqq bá šomást.
I admit.	qæbúl dáræm.
Surely.	hætmǽn.
Yes, my dear.	aré júnæm.
No.	xéyr.

It is not so.	intówr níst.
At all.	æbædǽn.
I don't agree.	qæbúl nǽdaræm.

Expressions of Time

before	píš
after	bǽ'd, pǽs
second	saniyé
next, future	ayændé
time	vǽqt (vǽxt)
once	yékbar
twice	dóbar
daily	ruzané
nightly	šæbané
twenty-four hours	šæbane rúz
weekly	hæftegí
monthly	maháne
annually	saláne
dusk	qorúb
this year	emsál
day by day	ruz be rúz
the day before yesterday	pærirúz

97

every other day	yek ruz dær miyún
every second day	do ruz dær miyún
before noon	piš æz zóhr
late in the afternoon	'æsr
midnight	nime šǽb
midnight	nesfe šǽb
the night after tomorrow	pæs færdá šǽb
Friday night	šæbe jom'é
hour to hour	sa'æt be sa'æt
office hours	sa'áte edarí
leap year	sale kæbisé
in a week's time	dær zærfe yek hafté
new year	sále nów
date of birth	taríxe tævvælód
late in fall	ævaxére pa'íz
early in spring	æva'éle bæhár
in time	be mowqé'
on time	sære sa'æt
every now and then	gah begáh
My watch is run down.	sa'æte mæn xabidǽ:st.
My watch is wrong.	sa'ætæm doróst kar némikone.

Your watch is fast by ten minutes.	sa'æte šomá dæh dæqiqé tónde.
Mina's watch is out of order.	sa'æte Mina xærábe.
Wind up the clock.	sa'æte divaríyo kúk kon.
It is time to go to bed.	væxte xábe.
Wait a minute.	ye dæqiqé sæbr kon.
Be quick.	zúd baš.
Your time is up.	væqte šomá tæmúm šód.

Fields of Study

medicine	pezeškí
pharmacy	darusazí
dentistry	dændanpezeškí
geology	zæmin-šenasí
astronomy	nojúm, setaré šenasí
banking	bankdarí
botany	giyah šenasí
education	amuzešo pærværéš
psychology	rævan šenasí
economics	eqtesád
natural sciences	'olúme tæbi'í
political sciences	'olúme siyasí

99

architecture	me'marí
fine arts	honærháye zibá
oriental studies	šærq šenasí
meteorology	hævá šenasí
nursing	pæræstarí
business administration	'olúme edarí
translation	tærjomé
philosophy	fælsæfé

Weather

climate	ab-o-hævá
changeable	motæqæyyér
continental	car fæslí
storm	tufán
fog	mǽh
frost	yæx bændán
hail	tagǽrg
I feel cold.	sǽrdæme.
I feel warm.	gǽrmæme.
It is two degrees of frost.	do dæræjé zire séfre.
It thunders (lightning).	rǽ'do bǽrq šod.
It has cleared up.	hævá baz šod.

The sun is shining again.	do baré aftáb šod.
It is windy.	bád míyad.
The wind is dropping down.	bád dare míxabe.
It is hailing.	tægǽrg míbare.
It is snowing.	bǽrf míyad.
It has snowed heavily.	bǽrfe sængíni nešæsté.

Professions

cook	ašpǽz
barber	sælmuní, arayešgǽr
maid	kolfǽt
waiter	pišxedmǽt
doorman	dærbún
shoe polisher	vaksí
shoemaker	kæffáš
driver	ranændé
judge	qazí
president	ræ'ís
assistant	dæstyár
writer	nevisændé
singer	xanændé
journalist	ruzname nevís

soldier	særbáz
police officer	æfsǽr
ambassador	sæfír
painter	næqqáš
poet	ša'ér
pilot	xælæbán
landlord	sabxuné

B. KEY TO THE EXERCISES AND SELF-TESTS

Pages 6-7, Exercise

1. Q	5. Q	9. S	13. Q
2. S	6. Q	10. Q	14. Q
3. Q	7. S	11. S	15. S
4. S	8. S	12. S	

Pages 16-18, Self-Test

Part 1A

1. 1	6. 2
2. 1	7. 2
3. 2	8. 1
4. 2	9. 1
5. 1	

Part 1B

1. A	6. B
2. B	7. B
3. B	8. B
4. A	9. A
5. A	10. B

Page 17, Vocabulary

1. student
2. eleven minutes to three
3. my friend
4. how
5. which friend of mine
6. handkerchief
7. good morning
8. good night
9. goodbye
10. goodbye

Page 17-18, True-False Questions

1. F	6. T	11. T	15. F
2. T	7. F	12. T	16. T
3. F	8. F	13. T	17. F
4. T	9. T	14. T	18. T
5. T	10. T		

Page 21, Pronunciation Drill 4

1. 1/3   3. 2/3   5. 1/2
2. 2/3   4. 2/3   6. 2/3

Page 32, Pronunciation Drill 5

1. 1   5. 4   9. 2
2. 2   6. 3   10. 1
3. 2   7. 2
4. 3   8. 3

Page 32, Pronunciation Drill 6

1. 4   5. 3   9. 2
2. 3   6. 2   10. 3
3. 4   7. 2   11. 4
4. 4   8. 2   12. 2

Pages 38 - 40, Self-Test

1. D   6. D
2. S   7. D
3. S   8. S
4. D   9. D
5. D   10. S

1. V   6. D   11. V   15. V
2. D   7. V   12. D   16. D
3. V   8. D   13. V   17. D
4. V   9. V   14. V   18. V
5. V   10. D

1. Good morning, Maryam.

2. Good morning, Parviz. How are you?

3. Not bad, thanks.

4. Excuse me, what is the name of this gentleman?

5. His name is Robert.

6. Does Robert study Persian or Arabic?

7. He studies Persian.

8. Does his friend study Persian also?

9. No. He studies Arabic.

10. Miss, where are you from?

11. I am an American.

12. Do you know Persian?

13. Yes, I know Persian a little.

14. Where is your professor from?

15. He is an Iranian.

16. Where is the Arabic professor from?

17. She is an Egyptian?

18. Does that lady know Arabic?

19. No. She doesn't know Arabic.

20. Does she know Persian?

21. Yes. She knows Persian well.

Page 40

1. D	6. D	11. B	15. D
2. B	7. D	12. C	16. A
3. C	8. C	13. A	17. B
4. A	9. D	14. D	18. D
5. B	10. C	15. C	20. C

Pages 56-58, Self-Test

1. danešjú	3	6. kucık	2
2. mišenasid	4	7. xaharášun	4
3. amriká	3	8. zæbanšenasí	5
4. almaní	3	9. zæbáne xarejí	6
5. engelísitun	5	10. ruznamehá	4

11. T	16. F
12. F	17. T
13. T	18. T
14. F	19. T
15. F	20. F

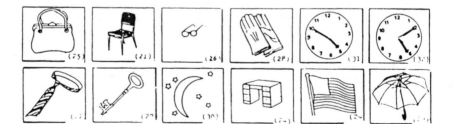

33. history   date

34. a watch   time

35. law   rights

36. Miss   lady

37. off   holiday

38. of   from

39. /ín qælǽm mále kiye?/

40. /ín kelidá mále šomást?/

41. /qælæmáye kí rúye míze?/

42. /zæbáne xarejíye šomá cíye?/

43. /šomá cǽnd zæbne xarejí mídunid?/

44. /be'æqidéye šomá 'æræbí æz engelisí sæxtǽre?/

45. /zæbáne madæríye soma cíye?/

46. /keláse 'ebrí tu ín saxtemúne?/

47. /bébæxšid aqá ketabxuné kojást?/

48. /bebæxšid xanóm be sa'æte šomá cǽnde?/

49. /pærcæme amriká cænd setaré dáre?/

50. /nešáne pærcǽme iran cíye?/

74-76 , Self-Test

	5. B	9. C	13. A
	6. C	10. A	14. B
	7. A	11. B	15. C
	8. B	12. C	

5 , True-False Questions

    4. T

    5. F

    6. T

107

Page 75 , Translation

1. My American friend.
2. Your Persian professor.
3. His English notebook.
4. Our Arabic class.
5. Your professor's home.
6. The fourth lesson.
7. The three-story building.
8. Room 33.
9. Near the window.
10. The university restaurant.
11. Good morning.
12. Goodbye.
13. His first name.
14. That is not right.
15. What date is it today?
16. What day is it today?
17. Sunday was a holiday.
18. The flag of Egypt.
19. The day after tomorrow.
20. Her brown handbag.

Page 76 , Vocabulary

1. worse
2. far
3. foreign language
4. light
5. cold
6. a little
7. humid
8. cloudy
9. to go

Pages 83 - 90 , Self-Test

1. D
2. S
3. D
4. D
5. D
6. D
7. D
8. S
9. D
10. D

108

11. Q	16. S
12. S	17. Q
13. Q	18. S
14. S	19. Q
15. S	20. Q

----

21. A/C	26. A/B
22. A/B	27. A/B
23. A/C	28. A/B
24. A/B	29. B/C
25. A/B	30. A/B

----

31. A	36. A
32. A	37. C
33. A	38. B
34. B	39. C
35. B	40. C

----

41. A	46. A
42. C	47. B
43. B	48. B
44. A	49. B
45. C	50. A

Pages 86-87, Vocabulary

1. C	5. D	9. B	13. A
2. A	6. C	10. B	14. C
3. D	7. C	11. B	15. D
4. C	8. D	12. D	

1. A	5. B
2. B	6. A
3. A	7. B
4. C	8. C

1. A	5. D
2. A	6. B
3. C	7. D
4. D	8. B

Page 88, Persian verbs/English verbs match

Persian	English
a.	he went
b.	I came
c.	he gave
d.	we would write, we used to write
e.	we see
f.	it was
g.	they had

h.	you are
i.	go!
j.	come!
k.	is
l.	they have
m.	I open
n.	please close
o.	you know
p.	he opens
q.	they close
r.	please read
s.	I know (somebody)
t.	it came, he came

Page 89, Present stems/Past stems match

Past stems	Present stems
a.	a
b.	r
c.	g
d.	nevis
e.	d
f.	xor
g.	hæst
h.	bin
i.	nešin
j.	bænd

Page 89 , Translation:

1. The Persian book.

2. I close

3. The window of the room.

4. I open.

5. His/her umbrella.

6. My friend's paper.

7. I study.

8. The English newspaper.

9. This paper.

10. I write.

Page 90 , Translation:

1. I study Persian at this university.

2. You study Persian in this class.

3. This lady knows English well.

4. She is a history professor.

5. That gentleman does not know Spanish.

6. You know him.

7. I am an American.

8. Our class was off yesterday.

9. You know this lad.

10. You now know Persian well.

A

about	dær baréye
accept (to)	qæbúl kærdǽn
actually	vaqe'ǽn, fe'lǽn
a lot	ziyád
abroad	xarejé
accountant	hesabdár
ache	dǽrd
address	nešaní
administration	edaré, ejrá
admit (to)	qæbúl kærdǽn
after	bǽ'd
afternoon	bæ'd æz zóhr
again	dobaré
against	dær bærabǽre
ago	píš, qǽbl
ahead	jeló, píš
air	hævá
airplane	hævapeymá
all	hæmé, hær
alone	tænhá
allow (to)	ejaze dadǽn, (....d)
almost	tæqribǽn
also	hǽm, hæmcenín
always	hæmišé
ambassador	sæfír

and	o, væ
annually	salané
answer	jæváb
anthropology	mærdom šenasí
any	híc, hær
anyone	kæsí, híckæs
approximately	tæqribǽn
Arabic	'æræbí
architecture	me'marí
arrive (to)	resídæn, (rés)
art	honǽr
ask (to)	porsidǽn, (pórs)
astronomy	setare šenasí, nojún
at	bé, dær, næzdíke
at last	belæxæré ·
aunt	xalé, 'æmmé
author	nevisændé
autumn	pa'iz

B

back	'æqǽb
bad	bǽd
bank	bánk
banking	bankdarí
barber	sælmuní, arayešgær
barley	jó

be able (to)	tunestæn, (tún)	breakfast	sobhané, nasta'í
because	cún, zíra	bring (to)	uvordæn, (ar)
become (to)	šodæn, (só)	brother	bæradær
bed	tæxtexáb	brown	qæhve'í ræng
before	píš æz	building	saxtemún
before noon	piš æz zóhr	burn (to)	suxtæn, (súz)
begin (to)	soru' kærdæn	bus	otobús
behind	'æqæb, poste sære	business	kár, kæsb
belong (to)	mále, motæ'ælléq budæn	but	væli, æmma
below	pa'íne, zíre	by	bá, bevæsiléye
best	behtarín		
better	behtær	C	
between	béyne, miyúne	call (to)	xundæn, (xún)
big	bozórg	can	tunestæn, (tún)
birth	tævællód	car	mašín, otomobíl
black	siyáh	carry (to)	bordæn, (bór)
blue	abí	catch a cold (to)	særma xordæn, (....xór)
board	tæxté		
boat	kestí, qayéq	center	mærkæz
body	bædæn	centeral	mærkæzí
book	ketáb	chair	sændælí
bookkeeping	ketabdarí	chalk	gæc
botany	giyah senasí	change	'ævæz kærdæn
both	hærdó	chemistry	šimí
boy	pesær	child	bæccé
bread	nún	cinema	sinemá
break (to)	sekæstæn, (sekæ)	city	šæhr

114

class	kelás, dæsté	**D**	
climate	ab-o-hævá	daily	ruzané
clock	sa'æte divarí	daily bread	ruzí
close	næzdík	Danish	danmarkí
close (to)	bæstǽn, (bǽnd)	dark	tiré
cloth	parcé	date	xormá
clothing	lebás	date	taríx (time)
coat	kót	date of birth	tarixe tævvælód
coffee	qæhvé	daughter	doxtǽr
cold	sǽrd	day after tomorrow (the)	pæs færdá
color	rǽng		
comb	šuné	day by day	ruz be rúz
come (to)	umædǽn, ('a)	deaf	kǽr
company	šerkǽt	dear	'æzíz
condition	hál, halǽt, væz'	deep	gówd, 'æmíq
continental	car fæsli, qare'í	degree	dæræjé
cook	ašpǽz	Denmark	danmárk
cook (to)	poxtǽn, (pǽz)	dentistry	dændán pezeskí
correct	doróst	desk	míze tæhrír
counseling	mæšverǽt	dialect	læhjé
country	kešvǽr	die (to)	mordǽn, (mír)
cream	sær šír, kerém (rǽng)	difficult	sæxt
		dig (to)	kændǽn, (kæn)
crowded	šulúq	dinner	šám
cup	fenjún	displeased	narazí
cut (to)	boridǽn, (bór)	do (to)	kærdǽn, (kón)
Cyprus	qebrés	doctor	doktór

door	dǽr	eleven	yazdǽh
doorman	dærbún	embassy	sefarǽt
down	pa'ín	employee	karmǽnd
draw (to)	kešidæn, (kéš)	end	entehá, axǽr
drill	tæmrín	end (to)	bepayán resanidǽ (....resán)
drink (to)	nušidæn, (núš)		
driver	ranændé	engineer	mohændés
drop (to)	oftadǽn, (óft)	entrust (to)	sepordǽn, (sepór
dry	xóšk	eraser	pakkón
dusk	qorúb	evening	šǽb
		every	hǽr

E

		every other day	yek ruz dær miyún
		every second day	do ruz dær miyún
each	hǽr	evil	bædí, bælá
each other	yekdigé, hæmdigé	examination	emtehán
ear	gúš	except	józ, qéyr æz
early	zúd	excuse	bæhané
east	mæšréq	excuse me	bébæxšid
eat (to)	xordǽn, (xór)	exercise	tæmrín
economics	eqtesád	eye	cešm
education	amuzeš -o-pærværéš	eyeglasses	'eynæk
effort (to make)	kušidæn, (kúš), kušeš kærdǽn		

		F	
Egyptian	mesrí		
eight	hǽst		
eighteen	hijdǽh	face	rú, suræt
eighty	hæstád	fall	pa'íz
electricity	bǽrq	fall off (to)	oftadǽn, (óft)
elementary school	dæbestán	familiar	ašná, xodemuní

116

family	famíl	forty	cél
family name	ésme famíl	four	cár
far	dúr	fourteen	cardǽh
father	pedǽr	French (language)	færansć
favor	lótf	Frenchman	færansæví
feel (to)	ehsás kærdǽn	Friday	jom'é
few	cænd, bǽ'zi	Friday night	jom'e šǽb
fifteen	punzdǽh	friend	dúst
fifty	pænjáh	from	æz
find (to)	peyda kærdǽn	frost	yæx bændán
fine	xúb	future	ayændé
fine arts	honærháye zibá		
Finland	fænlánd		
Finnish	fænlandí	**G**	
first	ævvǽl		
fish	mahí	garden	báq
five	pǽnj	garlic	sír
flag	pærcǽm	gentleman	aqá
flood	séyl	geography	joqrafí
floor	zæmín, kǽfe otáq	geology	zæmin šenasí
flower	gól	German	alamní
fog	mǽh	get (to)	gereftǽn, (gír)
foot	pá	get married (to)	ezdevaj kærdǽn
for	bæráye	girl	doxtǽr
force	nirú	give (to)	dadǽn, (d)
foreign	xarejí	glad	xošhál
forget (to)	færamúš kærdǽn	glass	šišé
fortunately	xošbæxtané	gloves	dæstkéš

117

go (to)	ræftǽn, (r)	head	sǽr
God	xodá	health	sælamætí
God willing	enša'ælláh	hear (to)	sǽnidæn, (seno)
gold	tælá, zǽr	heavy	sængín
golden	tæla'í	Hebrew	'ebrí
good	xúb	hello	sælám
good-bye	xoda haféz	high scrool	dæbirestán
grandfather	pedǽr bozórg	high school teacher	dæbír
grandmother	madǽr bozórg	history	taríx
great	bozórg	home	xuné
green	sǽbz	home economics	xanedarí
grey	xakestærí	honoring	tæšríf
group	gorúh	hotel	mehmunxuné
guardian	vælí	hour	sa'ǽt
guest	mehmún	hour to hour	sa'æt be sa'ǽt
		house	xuné, mænzél
		how	cetówr
H		how much/ how many	cǽnd
hail	tægǽrg	husband	šowhǽr
hair	mú	hundred	sǽd
half	ním, nésf	Hungary	mæjarestán
hand	dǽst		
handbag	kife dæstí		
handkerchief	dæstmál		
hard	sǽxt	**I**	
hat	koláh	I	mǽn
have (to)	daštǽn, (dár)	if	ǽge
he	ú	in	tú, dǽr

118

in a familiar way	xodemuní
in a good mood	sǽre hál
in a week's time	dǽr zǽrfe yek hǽfté
in front of	ruberúye, moqabéle
in time	be mowqé'
India	hénd, hendustán
Indian	hendí
inside	tú, daxél
instructor	mo'ællém, ostád
insurance	bimé
interesting	jalébe tævæjjóh
into	túye, dǽr
introduction	mo'ærrefí
Iranian	iraní
is not	níst
it	ún

J

Japan	zapón
Japanese	zaponí
job	kár
journalist	ruznamé nevís
judge	qazí
jump (to)	pæridǽn, (pǽr)
just	doróst, bejá

K

key	kelíd
kill (to)	koštǽn, (kóš)
kind	nów', mehræbán
kis (to)	busidǽn, (bús)
know (to)	dunestǽn, (dún)
Korea	koré
Korean	kore'í

L

lady	xanóm
landlord	sahebxuné
large	bozórg
last (to)	tul kešidǽn, (....kéš)
last	axær, gozæšté
last night	dišǽb
late	dír
late in the afternoon	'æsr
later	bæ'dǽn
laugh (to)	xændidǽn, (xǽnd)
law, rights	hoqúq
leap year	sale kæbisé
learn (to)	yad gereftǽn, (gír)
leave (to)	hærkǽt kærdǽn
left	cǽp

leg	pá	many times	barhá
lesson	dǽrs	married	motæ'æhéll
letter	namé	matter	mowzú'
library	ketabxuné	meaning	mæ'ní
library science	ketabdarí	medicine	pezeškí
Libya	libí	meteorology	hæva šenasí
lick (to)	lisidǽn, (lís)	Mexico	mekzík
life	zendegí	midnight	nésfe šæb, nime š
light	rowšæn, rowšæna'í núr	mild	molayém
		minute	dæqiqé
lightning	bǽrq	Miss	xanóm, dušizé
like	mésle, šæbíhe	mistake	dæqiqé
like (to)	dúst daštæn, (....dár)	Monday	do šæmbé
linguist	zæbán šenás	money	púl
linguistics	zæbán šenasí	monster	dív
lip	læb	month	máh
listen (to)	guš dadǽn, (.... d)	monthly	mahané
long	dæráz, tulaní	moon	máh
look (to)	negah kærdǽn	more	bištǽr
lose (to)	æz dæst dadǽn, gom kærdǽn	morning	sobh
		mostly	bištær, æsasǽn
		mother	madǽr
M		mother tongue	zæbáne madærí
		Mr.	aqá
magazine	mæjællé	Mrs.	xanóm
mail	póst	must	bayǽd
make (to)	saxtǽn, (sáz)		
many	xéyli, besyár		

120

N

name	ésm
natural science	'olume tæbi'í
navy blue	sorme'í
near	næzdík
necktie	keravát
nephew	bæradær zadéh
net	túr
never	hærgéz
new	nów, tazéh, jædíd
newspaper	ruznaméh
next	bæ'd, ayændé
nice	xúb, mehræbán
niece	doxtær æmmú
night	šæb
nightly	šæbané
nine	nóh
nineteen	nuzdǽh
ninety	nævǽd
no	næxéyr, næe
noon	zóhr
north	šomál
nose	biní
not at all	æbædǽn
note	yad dášt
notebook	dæftær
now	halá

number	šomaré, nomré
nurse	pæræstár
nursing	pæræstarí
occasionally	gáhi
occupation	šóql
of	æz
of course	ælbæté
off	dúr, jodá
office	edaré
office hours	sa'ate edarí
officer	æfsær
official	ræsmí
often	barhá, æqlæb
on	rúye
on time	sære væqt
once	yek bár
one	yék
open	báz
opinion	æqidé
or	yá
orange	narenjí (ræng)
order	tærtíb
orient	šǽrq
oriental	šǽrqí
oriental studies	šærq šenasí
other	digé
out of order	xæráb
outside	xaréj, birún

over here	injá	pleased	razí
over there	unjá	pleasure	tæfríh
owner	sahéb	post	póst
		poison	zæhr
P		Poland	lohestán
		police	polís
painter	næqqáš	political science	'olume siyasí
paper	kaqæz	pour (to)	rixtæn, (ríz)
park	párk	president	ræ'ís
park (to)	párk kærdæn	print	cáp
pass (to)	gozæštæn, (gozǽr)	professor	ostád
patr	ráh	property	má
pearl	dór, morvaríd	psychology	rævan šenasí
pen	qælǽm	purple	benæfš
pencil	medád	purse	kíf
people	mærdóm	put (to)	gozaštæn, (gozár)
perhaps	šáyæd	put on (to)	pušidæn, (púš)
permission	ejazé		
Persian	farsí		
pharmacy	dævaxuné	**Q**	
philosophy	fælsæfé		
phrase	'ebarær	quarter	rob'
physics	fizík	question	so'ál, porséš
pilot	xælæbán		
pink	surætí	**R**	
place	já		
plain	dæst	radio	radiyó
please	lotfǽn	rain	barún
		raw, uncooked	xám

122

really, by the way	rastí	search (to)	gǽštǽn, (gǽrd), jostejú kǽrdǽn
receive (to)	dǽryáft kǽrdǽn	season	fǽsl
recline	xǽm šodǽn, tekye dadǽn	seat	já, sǽndǽlí
red	sórx, qerméz	second	dovvóm
reply (to)	jǽváb dadǽn	secret	sérr, ráz
restaurant	resturán	secretary	monsí
return (to)	bǽr gǽštǽn, (....gǽrd)	see (to)	didǽn, (bín)
		self	xód
right	rást, doróst	sell (to)	foruxtǽn, (forúš)
road	ráh	send (to)	ferestadǽn, (ferést)
room	otáq	sentence	jomlé
round	gérd	seven	hǽft
route	ráh	seventeen	hivdǽh
run (to)	dǽvidǽn, (dó)	seventy	hǽftád
run down (to)	xabidǽn, ǽz kar oftadǽn, (.... óft)	sew (to)	duxtǽn, (dúz)
		shake (to)	tǽkán dadǽn, (....d)
S		sharp	tíz
safety	sǽlamǽt	shine (to)	dǽrǽxšidǽn, (dǽrǽš)
salt	nǽmǽk	ship	keští
salty	súr	shoe	kǽfš
sand	sén	shoe polisher	vaksí
Saturday	šǽmbé	shoemaker	kǽffáš
say (to)	goftǽn	silver	noqré
scene	sǽhné	singer	xanǽndé
school	mǽdresé	sister	xahǽr
sea	dǽryá	sit (to)	nešǽstǽn, (nešín)

123

six	šíš	study (to)	xundǽn, (xún), motal'e kærdǽn
sixteen	šunzdǽh		
sixty	šæst	summer	tabestún
sleep (to)	xabidǽn, (xáb)	Sunday	yekšæmbé
slow	ahesté	sunny	aftabí
small	kucík	surely	ælbæté, mosællæmæn
snow	bǽrf		
soldier	særbáz	Sweden	so'edí
son	pesǽr	syntax	nǽhv
soon	zúd		
sooner or later	dir ya zúd	**T**	
sorry	motæ'æsséf	table	míz
sound	sedá	taste (to)	cešidǽn, (céš)
south	jonúb	tea	cáy
speak (to)	hærf zædǽn, (.... zǽn)	teach (to)	dǽrs dadǽn, (....d)
spend (to)	gozærundǽn, (gozǽr)	teapot	qurí
		television	televiziyún
		telling	guyá
spring	bahár	ten	dǽh
stand (to)	istadǽn, (íst)	thanks	mérsi
star	setaré	thanks to God	ælhæmdolláh
stay (to)	mundǽn, (mún)	that	ún
steal (to)	dozdidǽn, (dózd)	these	iná
still	hænúz	thesis	resalé
stop (to)	istadǽn, (íst)	they	išún
storm	tufán	thick soup	áš
story	dastán, hekayǽt	think (to)	fékr kærdǽn
stroll (to)	gærdéš kærdǽn	thirteen	sizdǽh

124

thirty	sí	twelve	dævazdǽh
this	ín	twenty	bíst
those	uná	twenty four hours	yek šæbáne rúz
thou	tó	twice	do bár
thousand	hezár	two	dó
three	sé	two hundred	devíst
three hundred	sisæd	typist	mašin nevís
thunder	ræ'd		
Thursday	pænj šæmbé		
tie	keravát	U	
time	væqt		
to	bé	umbrella	cǽtr
today	emrúz	uncle	'æmmú, da'í
together	bahǽm	under	zíre
tomorrow	færdá	university	danešgáh
tongue	zæbán	until	tá
tonight	emšǽb	up	balá
too	hǽm, hæmcenín	Urdu	ordú
translate (to)	tærjomé kærdǽn		
translation	tærjomé	V	
translator	motærjém	very	xéyli
travel (to)	mósaferǽt kærdǽn	view	næzǽr, 'æqidé
tribe	qówm	voice	sedá
trip	sæfǽr		
tuberculosis	sél		
Tuesday	se šæmbé	W	
Turkish	torkí		
turn (to)	picidæn, (píc)	wait (to)	sæbr kærdǽn
		waiter	pišxedmǽt

wall	divár	with	bá
warm	gǽrm	with pleasure	ba kæmále méyl
watch	sa'ǽt	woman	zǽn
way	ráh	word	kælæmé
we	má	work	kár
weather	hævá	write (to)	nevéstǽn, (nevís)
Wednesday	car sæmbá	writer	nevisændé
weekly	hæftegí	wrong	estebáh, qælǽt
well	xúb bexubí		
west	mæqréb	**Y**	
wet	mærtúb		
what	cé, cí	year	sál
when	kéy	yellow	zǽrd
whenever	hær vǽqt	yes	bǽle, aré
where	ko já	yesterday	dirúz
which	kudúm	yet	hænúz
white	sefíd	yogurt	mást
who	kí	you	šomá
whole	hæmé, tæmúm	young	jæván
whose	male kí?	Your Excellency	jenabe'alí
why	céra		
wide	pǽhn		
wife	zǽn		
wind	bád		
wind up (to)	kuk kærdǽn		
windy	tufaní		
winter	zemestún		
wish	arezú		

Printed in the United States
60495LVS00003B/103-111

9 780884 325574